Knitting Blues
Strick-Blues

12 Strickprojekte | 12 Knitting Projects

© 2015 Ulrike Gronert und Dagmara Berztiss

Herstellung und Verlag: BoD – Books on Demand, Norderstedt

Fotograf: Arno Kohlem

ISBN 9-783739-214054

Die Deutsche Nationalbibliothek verzeichnet diese Publikation in der Deutschen Nationalbibliografie; detaillierte bibliografische Daten sind im Internet über www.dnb.de abrufbar.

www.stricknit.com stricKnit

Knitting Blues
Strick-Blues

12 Strickprojekte | 12 Knitting Projects

Ulrike Gronert
Dagmara Berztiss

Dieses Buch beinhaltet 12 Strickstücke, die jeweils aus einem Rechteck oder Quadrat entstanden sind. Kleidungsstücke (Poncho, Cape, Bolero, Jäckchen), Wohnaccessoires (Handtücher, Babydecke, Kissen) und modische Accessoires (Armstulpen, Pareo, Stola) werden in unterschiedlichen Stricktechniken und Schnitten gezeigt.

Allgemeine Strickkenntnisse werden vorausgesetzt. Benötigen Sie weiterführende Informationen, empfehlen wir, ein Stricklehrbuch, einen Wollladen Ihres Vertrauens oder das Videoangebot im Internet zu nutzen.

Die Autorinnen
Das Autorenduo Dagmara Berztiss und Ulrike Gronert wurde durch den Erfolg der ersten beiden Bücher angespornt. Ihre langjährigen Erfahrungen, ihr Ideenreichtum und die Lust am Ausprobieren lässt immer neue Modelle entstehen. Inzwischen treten die beiden unter dem Label *stricKnit* auf. Schon der Name läßt erahnen, dass die Anleitungen sowohl in Englisch, als auch in Deutsch vorliegen (*knit* bedeutet Stricken auf Englisch).

Ulrike ist die Inhaberin des Karlsruher Wollcafés Lana L8 (www.lanal8.de) und begeisterte Strickdesignerin.

Dagmara strickt schon sehr lange und liebt es, Neues auszuprobieren und so lange zu experimentieren, bis ein „perfektes" Modell entstanden ist, was auch entsprechend viel Auftrennen bedeutet!

Der Fotograf
Arno ist professioneller Fotograf, der viel durch die Welt gereist ist und jetzt in Karlsruhe wohnt. Unter *www. arnokohlem.com* können Sie seine Arbeiten anschauen.

Dank
Ein ganz besonderer Dank geht an unsere Models Insa und Uli, die der Sommerhitze und dem kalten Herbstwetter standgehalten haben.
Ebenso ein ganz besonderer Dank geht an unsere KorrekturleserInnen Ursula, Karen und Norbert, die die Fehler entdecken, die wir nicht mehr sehen.

Knitting instructions for 12 objects, each starting out as a rectangle or a square, are provided in this book. Wearable items (poncho, shrug, capelet, bolero), home items (blanket, pillow, towels, sitting pad) and accessories (pulse warmers, scarf, pareo) feature diverse knitting techniques and construction choices.

A general knowledge of knitting is assumed. For extra help, try a "How to..." knitting book, ask at your local yarn store (LYS) or check on the internet where videos are available for just about every knitting technique and method.

The authors
The authors Dagmara Berztiss and Ulrike Gronert have published two successful knitting pattern books. Years of knitting experience, lots of ideas and a desire to test them result in new patterns. The two now knit and design under the label *stricKnit*. As the name implies, the patterns are written in both English and German (*stricken* means knitting in German).

Ulrike is the owner of the yarn shop and cafe Lana L8 (*www.lanal8.de*) in Karlsruhe and is an enthusiastic designer.

Dagmara has been knitting for a long time. She likes to try new techniques and to experiment until the final perfect model is created — a lot of frogging is involved.

The photographer
Arno is a professional photographer who has traveled the world and now lives in Karlsruhe. His work can be seen under *www.arnokohlem.com*.

Thank you
Special thanks to our models Insa & Uli, who braved the extreme summer heat and cold fall weather. Thanks to Ursula, Karen and Norbert for proofreading and finding those mistakes we couldn't see anymore.

Inhalt / Contents

Idee / Idea

Was kann man alles aus einem Rechteck zaubern?

Diese Frage stellten wir uns zu Beginn unseres dritten Buches. Herausgekommen sind zwölf ganz unterschiedliche Modelle.

Ein Rechteck zu stricken, hört sich zunächst einfach an, doch kann das angewandte Strickmuster auch zur Herausforderung werden.

Einige Strickstücke in diesem Buch wurden als Rechteck oder Quadrat gestrickt und dann speziell gefaltet und zusammengenäht. Andere hingegen haben nach dem Stricken bereits die passende Form.

Bei manchen wurde das Rechteck nachträglich, z.B. durch das Anstricken von Ärmeln, in eine tragbare Form gebracht. Und schließlich gibt es auch Strickstücke, die aus mehreren Rechtecken und Quadraten zusammengesetzt wurden.

Der Titel des Buches „Knitting Blues" bezieht sich auf die vorherrschende Farbe der Modelle: blau. Falls Sie jedoch einen „Strick-Blues" haben, weil Sie nicht wissen was Sie stricken sollen, dann gibt Ihnen dieses Buch hoffentlich Anregungen.

Die Modellnamen bedeuten die Farbe BLAU in verschiedenen Sprachen. Ergänzend zu diesem Buch ist ein Wandkalender erschienen, der die 12 Strickstücke auf eine besondere Art in Szene setzt. Er ist im üblichen Fachhandel erhältlich.

Warum ist dieses Buch auf Deutsch und auf Englisch erschienen? Ganz einfach. Ulrike ist Deutsche, Dagmara Amerikanerin. Sie können entscheiden, welche Anleitung für Sie einfacher zu verstehen ist, oder aber Sie lernen. Anleitungen in beiden Sprachen zu lesen.

In this, our third knitting pattern book, we wanted to challenge ourselves and develop a wide variety of patterns to knit. The challenge — what can be made from a simple RECTANGLE? As it turns out, a lot!

A simple rectangle doesn't mean a simple pattern — although it can.

Many objects in the book are knit as a single rectangle and you're done! Other objects are knit as a single rectangle and then folded and sewn to produce the finished object.

Still others have additions to transform the rectangle into a wearable object, e.g., knitting on sleeves. And finally there are objects made up of a number of different squares and rectangles and then knit or sewn together.

The book is called *Knitting Blues* because the knit objects are predominantly blue. If you have the knitting blues because you don't know what to knit, maybe you can find something special in this book — it doesn't have to be blue.

The names of the patterns mean the color BLUE in twelve different languages. In addition to the book, a wall calendar displaying the twelve knit objects in original ways is available where calendars are sold.

The patterns are written in German and English simply because Ulrike is German and Dagmara is American — you decide which pattern is easier to follow or you can learn knitting terms in another language.

Allgemeines / General Info

Größe

Jedes Modell ist in jeweils einer Größe beschrieben. Meistens handelt es sich um eine Einheitsgröße.

Ist eine Größenanpassung sinnvoll, finden Sie genaue Angaben, wie die Größe variiert werden kann. Keine Angst, das geht ganz einfach, denn wir stricken ja lediglich Rechtecke.

Abkürzungen

Leider gibt es keine international üblichen Abkürzungen für Strickanleitungen. Deshalb findet man in jeder Veröffentlichung unterschiedliche Bezeichnungen. Alle in diesem Buch verwendeten Abkürzungen finden Sie auf der letzten Seite. Zudem werden dort die geläufigsten Strickmuster und häufig benutzte Stricktechniken erklärt. Benutzen wir spezielle Abkürzungen/Strickmuster, die nur ein Modell betreffen, werden diese direkt in der Anleitung erklärt.

Maschenprobe

Oft gehasst, aber doch sehr wichtig. Nehmen Sie sich Zeit, eine korrekte Maschenprobe zu ermitteln. Falls Ihre Maschenprobe zu viele Maschen oder Reihen aufweist, verwenden Sie bitte dickere Nadeln. Haben Sie weniger Maschen oder Reihen als angegeben, verwenden Sie bitte dünnere Nadeln.

Sizes

Only one size is provided for each object — in many cases, one size fits most.

For some wearable pieces, the size can easily be adjusted and instructions on how to do so are given. Don't worry - it's easy to change! They are, after all, just squares and rectangles!

Abbreviations

Unfortunately, there are no universal abbreviations for knitting patterns and different publications have different norms. All abbreviations used in this book in German and English are listed in a chart on the last page. In addition, the chart lists short explanations of knitting terms used in this book. If an abbreviation or stitch is only used in one pattern, this is noted directly in the pattern.

Gauge

Please take the time to make sure your gauge is correct. If you have too many stitches or too many rows, switch to a larger needle. If you have too few stitches or too few rows, switch to a smaller needle.

mawaawa

Ein kuscheliges und bequemes Jäckchen für die kalten Tage. Zunächst wird ein großes Quadrat gestrickt, dann gefaltet und zusammengenäht. Zum Schluss noch Ärmel dran, und fertig ist das Lieblingsstück.

The shrug is first worked as a large square. Folding and sewing results in a very warm, snug and comfortable shoulder shrug for chilly days. The arms are knit on afterwards.

Malou Lang Yarns 65m (71yd) / 50g
70% Alpaka, 20% Polyamid, 10% Schurwolle
70% alpaca, 20% nylon, 10% wool

Endgröße 95 x 95 cm.

Measurements 95 x 95 cm (37.4").

Material Malou, 11 Knäuel Fb. 10.

Yarn *Malou*, 11 skeins #10.

Nadeln Rundstricknadel 8 mm, 100 cm lang und ein Nadelspiel 8 mm.

Needles 8 mm: circular 100 cm (40"), set of double pointed (dp).

Maschenprobe 11,5 M x 18 R = 10 x 10 cm im Grundmuster.

Gauge 11.5 sts and 18 rows = 10 cm (4") in diagonal body pattern.

Muster
Perlmuster (PM) (ungerade Maschenzahl)
Jede R *1 M re, 1 M li; von * wdh, 1 M re.

Stitches
Seed stitch (odd number of sts)
Every row *k1, p1, rep from *, k1.

1/1 Rippenmuster in Runden (gerade Maschenzahl)
Jede R *1 M re, 1 M li; von * wdh.

1/1 Rib in the round (even number of sts)
Every row *k1, p1, rep from *.

Grundmuster Körperteil (teilbar durch 18 M) – siehe Diagramm.

Diagonal body pattern (multiple of 18 sts) - see diagram.

Es werden immer 9 M glatt rechts (gr) und 9 M im Perlmuster (PM) gestrickt. Damit es diagonale Streifen gibt, werden in jeder Reihe die Muster um 1 Masche in die gleiche Richtung versetzt.
Reihen 1 - 18 wdh.

In every pattern repeat, 9 stitches in St st and 9 stitches in seed stitch are worked. In order to make the diagonal stripes, the pattern is shifted by one stitch in **every** row.
Rep rows 1 - 18 for pattern.

Anleitung Körperteil
101 M anschlagen und im Grundmuster mit einer Rückreihe beginnen. Dazu die Maschen wie folgt einteilen:
R 1 (RR): RM, *9 M li, 4 x (1 M re, 1 M li), 1 M re, von * 4-mal wdh, 9 M li, RM.
R 2 (HR): RM, 1 M li, 8 M re, *5 x (1 M re, 1 M li), 8 M re, von * 4-mal wdh, 1 RM.
R 3 (RR): RM, *7 M li, 4 x (1 M re, 1 M li), 1 M re, 2 M li, von * 4-mal wdh, 7 M li, 1 M re, 1 M li, RM.
Entsprechend der Strickschrift im Diagramm weiterarbeiten. So lange stricken, bis 9 Knäuel nahezu verbraucht sind und das Muster mit

For the body
Cast on 101 sts and work the diagonal body pattern beginning with a WS row as follows:
Row 1 (WS) ES, *p9, (k1, p1) 4 times, k1, rep from * 4 times, p9, ES.
Row 2 (RS) ES, p1, k8, *(k1, p1) 5 times, k8, rep from * 4 times, ES.
Row 3 ES, p7, *(k1, p1) 4 times, k1, p2, rep from * 4 times, p7, k1, p1, ES.
Continue in pattern following the diagram. Work until 9 skeins are almost used ending with Row 9 (after 8.5 pattern repeats). Bind off all stitches loosely in pattern.

der 9. Reihe (entspricht 8,5 Höhenrapporten) beendet wird. Alle Maschen locker im Muster abketten.

Ausarbeitung
Quadrat in der Mitte falten, so dass A auf A und B auf B liegen. Nun mit dem Matratzenstich die Seiten zwischen A und B zunähen, bis noch ca. 16 cm bis zum Umbruch offen sind.

Ärmel
Mit einem neuen Knäuel aus der seitlichen Öffnung mit dem Nadelspiel insg. 32 M aufnehmen. Nun zunächst 1 Runde re stricken und danach in 1/1 Rippenmuster übergehen. Solange stricken, bis das Knäuel zu Ende geht. Alle M locker im Muster abketten. Das gleiche nochmals auf der anderen Seite stricken. Zum Schluss alle Fäden vernähen.

Finishing
Fold the square in half so that the right sides are facing outwards, points A meet and points B meet. Using a mattress stitch, sew the sides closed between A and B so that the armhole is about 16 cm (6.3") long – see diagram.

Sleeves (make 2)
With dp needles and a new skein of yarn, pick up and knit 32 stitches along the armhole opening. Working in the round, knit one row. Begin 1/1 Rib and work until the skein is almost used up. Bind off in pattern. Weave in ends.

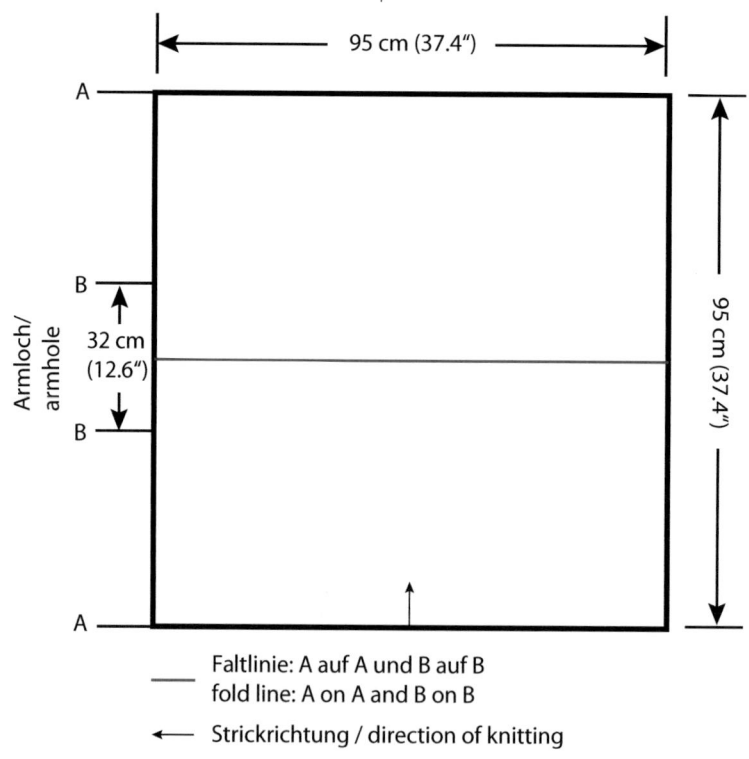

95 cm (37.4")

A

95 cm (37.4")

B

32 cm (12.6")

B

Armloch/ armhole

A

___ Faltlinie: A auf A und B auf B
fold line: A on A and B on B

⟵ Strickrichtung / direction of knitting

	-										-		-		-		-		-									18
17	-		-	-	-	-	-	-	-	-	-		-		-		-		-		-	-	-	-	-	-	-	
	-		-										-		-		-		-		-							16
15	-		-		-	-	-	-	-	-	-	-	-		-		-		-		-		-	-	-	-	-	
	-		-		-										-		-		-		-		-					14
13	-		-		-		-	-	-	-	-	-	-	-	-		-		-		-		-		-	-	-	
	-		-		-		-										-		-		-		-		-			12
11	-		-		-		-		-	-	-	-	-	-	-	-	-		-		-		-		-		-	
	-		-		-		-		-										-		-		-		-		-	10
9	-		-		-		-		-		-	-	-	-	-	-	-	-	-		-		-		-		-	
			-		-		-		-		-										-		-		-		-	8
7	-	-	-		-		-		-		-		-	-	-	-	-	-	-	-	-		-		-		-	
					-		-		-		-		-										-		-		-	6
5	-	-	-	-	-		-		-		-		-		-	-	-	-	-	-	-	-	-		-		-	
							-		-		-		-		-										-		-	4
3	-	-	-	-	-	-	-		-		-		-		-		-	-	-	-	-	-	-	-	-		-	
									-		-		-		-		-										-	2
1	-	-	-	-	-	-	-	-	-		-		-		-				-	-	-	-	-	-	-	-	-	

18 M Rapport, stets wdh. /
18 st repeat

	re M / k
-	li M / p

bibire

Das lange Rechteck aus glatt rechten und glatt linken Reihen sowie 2 unterschiedlichen Garnen kann durch Anbringen von Druckknöpfen auf unterschiedliche Weisen getragen werden. Spannend wird das Spiel aus horizontalen und vertikalen Strukturen, je nach Tragevariante.

A long rectangle is knit using stockinette and reverse stockinette stitch alternating between two different yarns. Horizontal or vertical stripes — or a mixture of both — emerge depending on the placement of snap closures and the way the piece is worn.

40 % Wolle, 25 % Seide, 25 % Polyamid, 10 % Mohair
40% wool, 25% silk, 25% nylon, 10% kid mohair
Valentina Bremont 200m (218yd) / 50g
60 % Alpaka, 40 % Wolle
60% alpaca, 40% wool

Endgröße 55 x 130 cm (ungespannt). Die Größe des Schulterwärmers ist einfach zu variieren. Die Breite des Rechtecks sollte ca. die Rückenlänge + 10 cm sein. Die Länge sollte ca. Körpergröße – 45 cm betragen

Material Silk Garden 4-ply, 4 Knäuel Fb. 373 (**A**); Valentina, 4 Stränge Fb. 5016 (**B**). Druckknöpfe.

Nadeln Rundstricknadel 3 mm, 60 cm lang.

Maschenprobe 21 M x 46 R = 10 x 10 cm im Muster (ungedehnt).

Tipp Die Fäden nicht abschneiden, sondern am Rand mit hochführen.

Musterabfolge
4 R gr mit **A** (1 R re, 1 R li, 1 R re, 1 R li).
6 R gl mit **B** (Achtung: die erste Reihe (eine HR) wird immer rechts gestrickt. Dadurch gibt es auf der Vorderseite keine Farbübergänge. (2 R re, 1 R li, 1 R re, 1 R li, 1 R re).
Reihen 1 – 10 stets wdh.

Anleitung
130 M mit **B** anschlagen und 6 R gl stricken. Dabei mit einer HR beginnen. Ab jetzt so lange immer in der obigen Musterabfolge stricken, bis das Strickstück lang genug ist oder das 4. Knäuel **A** aufgebraucht ist. Nach den letzten 6 Reihen mit **B** alle M locker abketten.

Fertigstellung
Alle Fäden vernähen und das Strickstück nicht spannen! Nun nach Belieben oder entsprechend dem Diagramm und Fotos die Druckknöpfe annähen. Je nach Knöpfung ergeben sich unterschiedliche Tragemöglichkeiten.

Measurements 55 x 130 cm (21.5 x 52") — unblocked. The size of the piece is easy to adjust. The width of the rectangle should be the length of your back **plus** 10 cm (4"). The length should be your height **minus** 45 cm (17.5").

Material *Silk Garden 4-ply*, 4 skeins #373 (**A**); *Valentina*, 4 skeins #5016 (**B**).

Notions snap closures.

Needles 3 mm: circular 60 cm (24").

Gauge 21 sts and 46 rows = 10 cm (4") in pattern (unstretched).

Note Rather than cut the yarn at color changes, carry the unused yarn up the side.

Yarn & pattern sequence
With **A**, work 4 rows St st.
Change to **B**. Knit one row. Starting with a WS row, work 5 rows in rev St st.
Repeat rows 1 - 10 for pattern.

Instructions
With **B**, cast on 130 sts. Beginning with a RS row, work 6 rows in rev St st. Work yarn & pattern sequence until the piece is long enough or 4 skeins of **A** have been used. Work last 6 rows of **B** in pattern and bind off all stitches loosely.

Finishing
Weave in ends. DO NOT BLOCK. Sew on snap closures as desired for alternative ways to wear as shown in the diagram and on the photos.

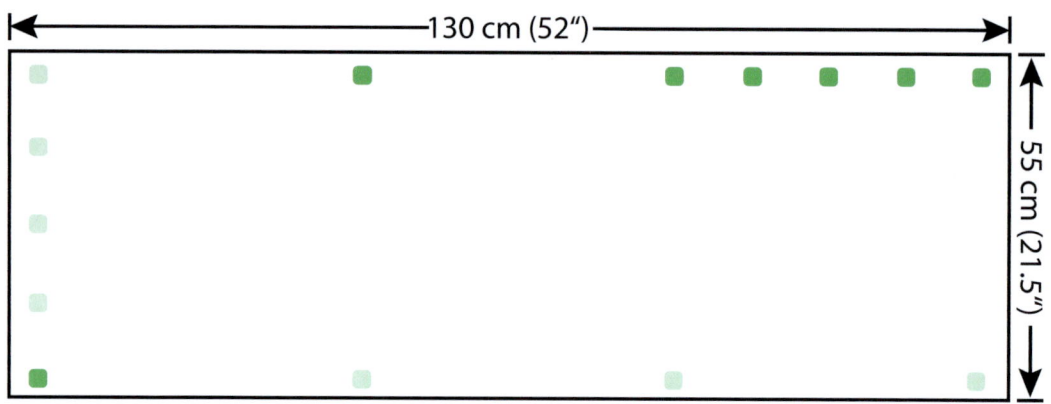

←————————130 cm (52")————————→

55 cm (21.5")

Druckknöpfe / snap fasteners

okchakko

Die Stulpen werden mit einem weichen, luxuriösen Garn in Runden gestrickt. Horizontale Biesen sorgen für zusätzliche Wärme und einen interessanten Look.

The pulse warmers are knit in the round using a luxurious soft yarn. Horizontal tucks throughout add interest and extra warmth.

Sophie de Luxe Bremont 83m (90yd) / 25g
70 % Alpaka, 20 % Seide, 10% Kaschmir
70% alpaca, 20% silk, 10% cashmere

Endgröße 17 cm Umfang x 19 cm Länge.

Material Sophie de Luxe, 2 Knäuel Fb. 2109.

Nadeln kurzes Nadelspiel 3mm, 1 dünnere kurze Hilfsnadel.

Maschenprobe 24 M x 36 R = 10 x 10 cm in gr.

Grundmuster glatt rechts (gr) in Runden alle M re.

Biesen
Biesen sind Querfalten, die entstehen wenn die Maschen mit tieferliegenden Maschen zusammengestrickt werden. Hier werden immer 5 M „verbiest". D.h. mit der Hilfsnadel werden 5 Reihen unterhalb der zu verbiesenden Maschen 5 M aus der Rückseite aufgenommen. Man dreht das Strickstück so hin, dass man die Rückseite gut sieht. Nun werden von der Masche auf der Nadel direkt 5 Reihen nach unten gezählt. Dieser linke „Knubbel" wird nun auf die Hilfsnadel genommen (richtig in das Gestrick stechen und „Knubbel" auffädeln). In der gleichen Reihe bleiben und noch weitere 4 M auf die Hilfsnadel aufnehmen. Nun die Hilfsnadel hinter die eigentliche Nadel legen und die Maschen beider Nadeln zusammenstricken (immer 1 M von eigentlicher Nadel und 1 M von der Hilfsnadel zusammenstricken).

Anleitung (2-mal stricken)
44 M anschlagen und gleichmäßig auf alle 4 Nadeln verteilen (je 11 M) und zur Runde schließen, so dass die M nicht verdreht werden. 6 R stricken.
Ab jetzt werden in jeder 6. Reihe 2-mal 5 M verbiest (vb). Diese liegen sich gegenüber und werden immer versetzt. Alle nicht betroffenen Maschen werden re gestrickt!
Achtung: in den Runden 49/50, 79/80 und

Measurements 17 cm (6.7") circumference; 19 cm (7.5") long.

Yarn *Sophie de Luxe*, 2 skeins #2109.

Needles 3mm: set of short double-pointed (dp); cable needle or other short needle smaller than 3 mm.

Gauge 24 sts and 36 rows = 10 cm (4") in St st.

Basic pattern St. st. In the round, all stitches are knit.

Horizontal tuck (HT)
Tucks are formed when the same number of stitches are knit together with stitches a few rows below. For these pulse warmers, 5 stitches are picked up from the wrong side with a separate needle 5 rows below the current row. Here's how it works. Adjust the work so that you can see the wrong side. Now count 5 rows directly below your current stitch. Work the extra needle through the purl bump. While staying in the same row, place next 4 sts (purl bumps) onto the extra needle. Place the extra needle parallel to the working needle and knit the first st from each needle together. Work same for other 4 sts.

Instructions (make 2)
Cast on 44 sts and distribute evenly over 4 dp needles (11 sts per needle). Join round being careful not to twist sts. Knit 6 rounds.
Starting now and in every 6th round 5 st will be tucked twice. The tucks are evenly distributed within one round and shifted every 6th round. All other stitches and rounds are knit. Take special care in rounds 49/50, 79/80 and 91/92 where the horizontal tucks are carried

91/92 werden die Biesen über den Rundenanfang hinweg gestrickt.

R 7: 5 M vb, 17 M re, 5 M vb, 17 M re.
R 13: 11 M re, 5 M vb, 17 M re, 5 M vb, 6 M re.
R 19: 3 M re, 5 M vb, 17 M re, 5 M vb, 14 M re.
R 25: 14 M re, 5 M vb, 17 M re, 5 M vb, 3 M re.
R 31: 6 M re, 5 M vb, 17 M re, 5 M vb, 11 M re.
R 37: 17 M re, 5 M vb, 17 M re, 5 vb.
R 43: 9 M re, 5 M vb, 17 M re, 5 M vb, 8 M re.
R 49: 20 M re, 5 M vb, 17 M re, 2 M vb.
R 50: 3 M vb, 41 M re.
R 55: 12 M re, 5 M vb, 17 M re, 5 M vb, 5 M re.
R 61: 1 M re, 5 M vb, 17 M re, 5 M vb, 16 M re.
R 67: 15 M re, 5 M vb, 17 M re, 5 M vb, 2 M re.
R 73: 4 M re, 5 M vb, 17 M re, 5 M vb, 13 M re.
R 79: 18 M re, 5 M vb, 17 M re, 4 M vb.
R 80: 1 M vb, 43 M re.
R 85: 7 M re, 5 M vb, 17 M re, 5 M vb, 10 M re.
R 91: 21 M re, 5 M vb, 17 M re, 1 M vb.
R 92: 4 M vb, 40 M re.
R 97: 10 M re, 5 M vb, 17 M re, 5 M vb, 7 M re.
R 103: 2 M re, 5 M vb, 17 M re, 5 M vb, 15 M re.
R 109: 13 M re, 5 M vb, 17 M re, 5 M vb, 4 M re.

In nächster Runde alle M locker abketten. Fäden vernähen. Stulpen nicht spannen!

over to the next round.

Row 7 5 st HT, k17, 5 st HT, k17.
Row 13 k11, 5 st HT, k17, 5 st HT, k6.
Row 19 k3, 5 st HT, k17, 5 st HT, k14.
Row 25 k14, 5 st HT, k17, 5 st HT, k3.
Row 31 k6, 5 st HT, k17, 5 st HT, k11.
Row 37 k17, 5 st HT, k17, 5 st HT.
Row 43 k9, 5 st HT, k17, 5 st HT, k8.
Row 49 k20, 5 st HT, k17, 2 st HT.
Row 50 3 st HT, k41.
Row 55 k12, 5 st HT, k17, 5 st HT, k5.
Row 61 k1, 5 st HT, k17, 5 st HT, k16.
Row 67 k15, 5 st HT, k17, 5 st HT, k2.
Row 73 k4, 5 st HT, k17, 5 st HT, k13.
Row 79 k18, 5 st HT, k17, 4 st HT.
Row 80 1 st HT, k43.
Row 85 k7, 5 st HT, k17, 5 st HT, k10.
Row 91 k21, 5 st HT, k17, 1 st HT.
Row 92 4 st HT, k40.
Row 97 k10, 5 st HT, k17, 5 st HT, k7.
Row 103 k2, 5 st HT, k17, 5 st HT, k15.
Row 109 k13, 5 st HT, k17, 5 st HT, k4.

Loosely bind off stitches and weave in ends.
DO NOT BLOCK!

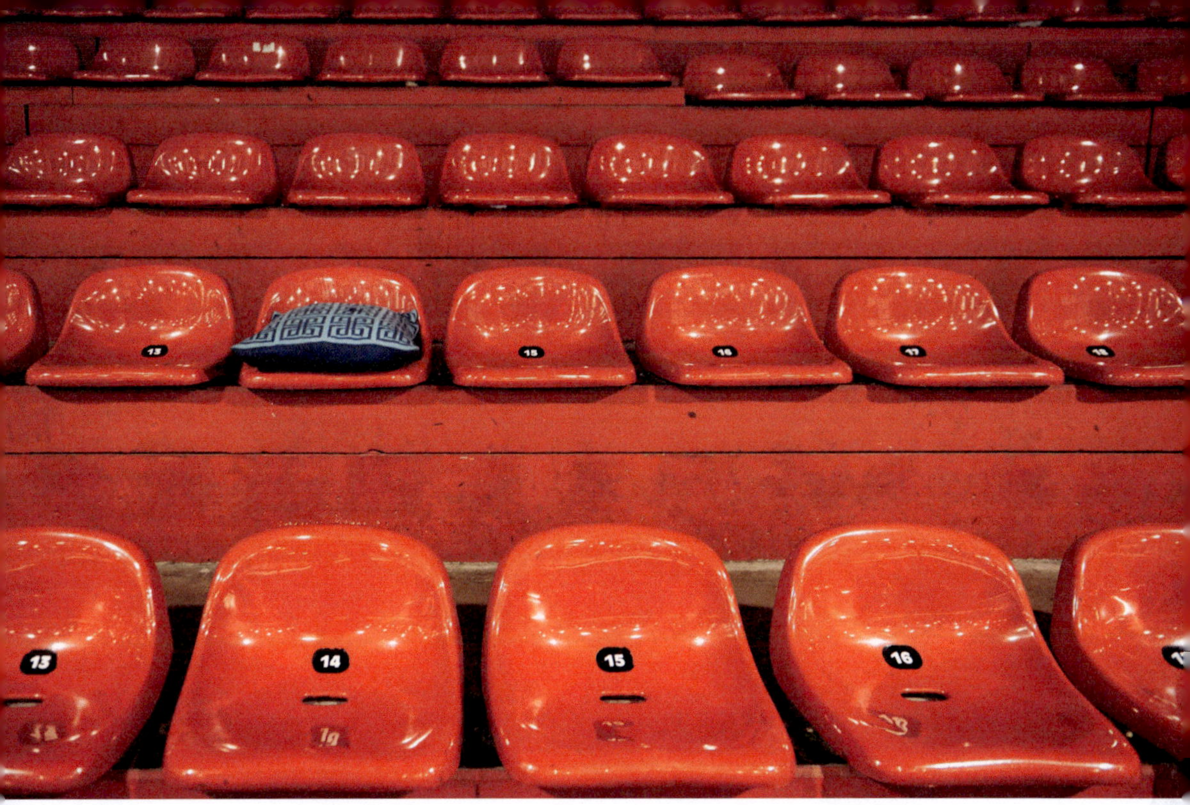
13
14
15
16

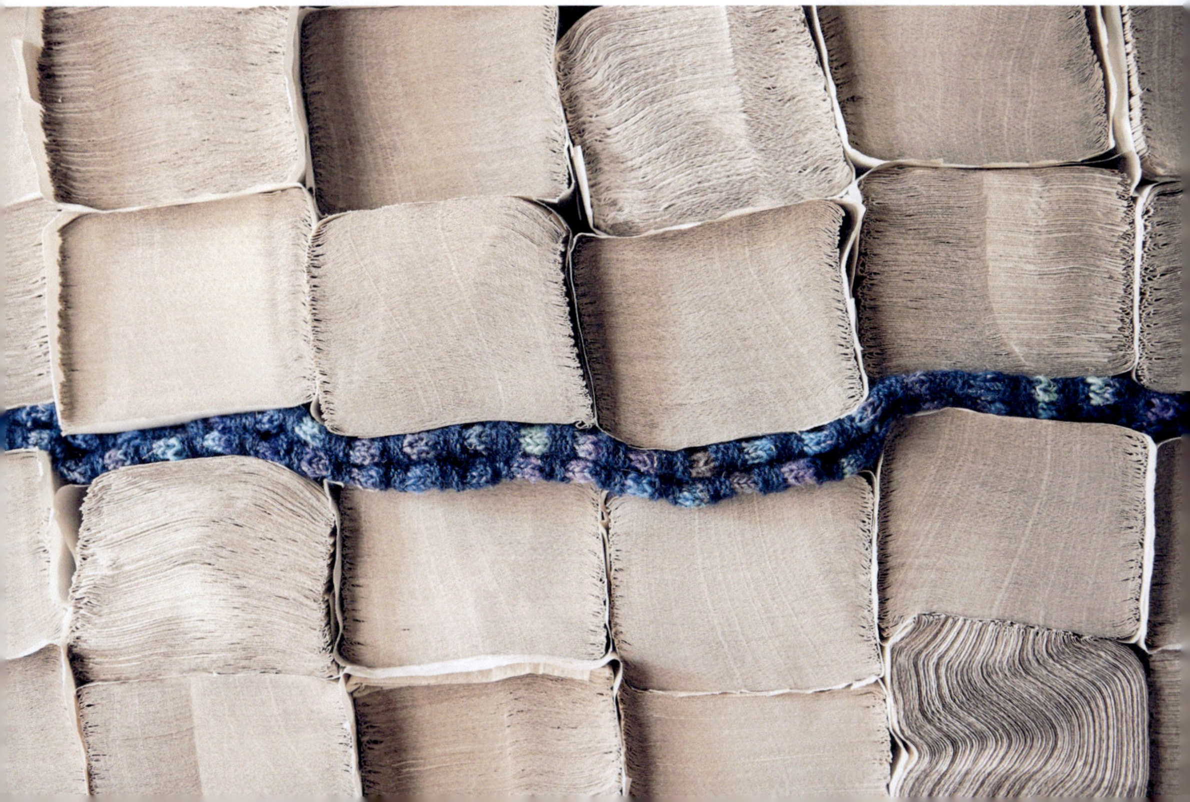

wu

Der Poncho kann auf unterschiedliche Arten getragen werden, so dass immer ein neuer Look entsteht. Er wird komplett an einem Stück gestrickt und mit dem breiten Rückenteil begonnen. Ist dieses lang genug, wird das Strickstück in der Mitte geteilt und die beiden Vorderteile getrennt fertig gestrickt.

The poncho, which can be worn in many different ways, is knit as one piece starting with the back. When the back is long enough, the piece is divided in two and each of the front pieces are knit separately.

Novena Lang Yarns 110m (120yd) / 25g
50 % Wolle, 30% Alpaka, 20 % Polyamid
50% wool, 30% alpaca, 20% nylon

Endgröße 80 cm breit x 165 cm lang.

Material Novena, 14 Knäuel Fb. 6.
Nadeln Rundstricknadel 5 mm, 100 cm lang.
Hilfsnadel.
Maschenprobe 21 M x 30 R = 10 x 10 cm in gr.

Muster
Windmühle (WiM) (teilbar durch 16 M)
Das Muster ist eine Kombination aus Loch- und Zopfmuster. Das Zopfmuster besteht aus 2 unterschiedlichen Drehungen:

3 M nach rechts verzopfen (3/3 M rz):
3 M auf Hilfsnadel abh und hinter die Arbeit legen, 3 M re, dann die 3 M von der Hilfsnadel re stricken.
3 M nach links verzopfen (3/3 M lz):
3 M auf Hilfsnadel abh und vor die Arbeit legen, 3 M re, dann die 3 M von der Hilfsnadel re stricken.

Entsprechend Strickschrift stricken oder:
R 1: 3 M re, U, 1 ÜZA, 6 M re, 2 Mrezus, U, 3 M re.
Alle geraden R: alle M und U li.
R3: 2 M re, 2 x (U, 1 ÜZA), 4 M re, 2 x (2 Mrezus, U), 2 M re.
R 5: 1 M re, 3 x (U, 1 ÜZA), 2 M re, 3 x (2 Mrezus, U), 1 M re.
R7: 2 M re, 3 x (U, 1 ÜZA), 3 x (2 Mrezus, U), 2 M re.
R 9: 5 M re, 1 x 3/3 M rz, 5 M re.
R 11: 2 M re, 2 x 3/3 M lz, 2 M re.
R 13: 2 M re, 2 Mrezus, U, 1 M re, 1 x 3/3 M rz, 1 M re, 1 U, 1 ÜZA, 2 M re.
R 15: 1 M re, 3 x (2 Mezus, U), 2 M re, 3 x (U, 1 ÜZA), 1 M re.
R 17: 3 x (2 Mezus, U), 4 M re, 3 x (U, 1 ÜZA).
R 19: 1 M re, 2 x (2 Mezus, U), 6 M re, 2 x (U, 1 ÜZA), 1 M re.

Measurements 80 cm wide x 165 cm long (31.5 x 65").

Yarn *Novena*,14 skeins #6.
Needles 5 mm: circular 100 cm (40").
Notions cable needle.
Gauge 21 sts and 30 rows = 10 cm (4") in St st.

Stitches
Windmill (WM) (multiple of 16 sts)
The pattern is a combination of cable and openwork stitches. The cable pattern uses two different twists:

6 st right cable (C6B)
Place 3 sts on a cable needle and hold to **back** of work, k3, k3 from cable needle.
6 st left cable (C6F)
Place 3 sts on a cable needle and hold to **front** of work, k3, k3 from cable needle.

Follow either the chart or the following directions:
Row 1 k3, yo, skp, k6, k2tog, yo, k3.
Row 2 and all even rows purl.
Row 3 k2, (yo, skp) twice, k4, (k2tog, yo) twice, k2.
Row 5 k1, (yo, skp) 3 times, k2, (k2tog, yo) 3 times, k1.
Row 7 k2, (yo, skp) 3 times, (k2tog, yo) 3 times, k2.
Row 9 k5, C6B, k5.
Row 11 k2, C6F twice, k2.
Row 13 k2, k2tog, yo, k1, C6B, k1, yo, skp, k2.
Row 15 k1, (k2tog, yo) 3 times, k2, (yo, skp) 3 times, k1.
Row 17 (k2tog, yo) 3 times, k4, (yo, skp) 3 times.
Row 19 k1, (k2tog, yo) twice, k6, (yo, skp) twice, k1.
Row 21 k2, k2tog, yo, k8, yo, skp, k2.
Repeat rows 1 - 22 for pattern.

R 21: 2 M re, 2 Mezus, U, 8 M re, U, 1 ÜZA, 2 M re.
Reihen 1-22 wdh.

Anleitung
163 M anschlagen und 10 Reihen kr stricken. Die
nächsten 10 Reihen wie folgt stricken:
1 RM, 5 M kr, 151 M gr, 5 M kr, 1 RM.

Danach wie folgt stricken:
22 R: 1 RM, 5 M kr, *16 M WiM, 11 M gr, von *
5-mal wiederholen, 16 M WiM, 5 M kr, 1 RM.
12 R: 1 RM, 5 M kr, 151 M gr, 5 M kr, 1 RM.
22 R: 1 RM, 5 M kr, 14 M gr, *16 M WiM, 11 M gr,
von * 4-mal wdh, 16 M WiM, 13 M gr, 5 M kr, 1 RM.
12 R: 1 RM, 5 M kr, 151 M gr, 5 M kr, 1 RM.
Die oben beschriebenen 68 Reihen insg. 3-mal
stricken.

In der folgenden Reihe wird der hintere Teil des
Halses vorbereitet. Dazu wie folgt stricken:
1 RM, 5 M kr, 16 M WiM, 11 M gr, 16 M WiM, 11 M
gr, 16 M WiM, 1 M Qzu, 11 M kr, 16 M WiM, 11 M gr,
16 M WiM, 11 M gr, 16 M WiM, 5 M kr, 1 RM.
Die nächsten 9 R: 1 RM, 5 M kr, 16 M WiM, 11 M
gr, 16 M WiM, 11 M gr, 16 M WiM, 12 M kr, 16 M
WiM, 11 M gr, 16 M WiM, 11 M gr, 16 M WiM, 5 M
kr, 1 RM.
In der nächsten Reihe (= 11 Musterreihe) wird die
Teilung vollzogen. Ab hier werden beide Vorderteile getrennt voneinander fertiggestrickt. Reihe
wie folgt arbeiten:
1 RM, 5 M kr, 16 M WiM, 11 M gr, 16 M WiM, 11 M
gr, 16 M WiM, 5 M kr, 1 RM; neuen Faden ansetzen
und das gleiche nochmal stricken.

Jedes Vorderteil hat nun 82 M und wird nach dem
gleichen Prinzip wie das Rückenteil gestrickt. D.h.
die nächsten 11 Reihen haben folgende Einteilung:
1 RM, 5 M kr, *16 M WiM, 11 M gr, von * 2-mal
wdh, 16 M WiM, 5 M kr, 1 RM.

Instructions
Cast on 163 sts and work 10 rows in garter st.
Work the next 10 rows as follows: ES, 5 g st, 151 St
st, 5 g st, ES.

Then work as follows over 68 rows:
22 rows: ES, 5 g st, *16 st WM, 11 St st, rep from *
5 times, 16 st WM, 5 g st, ES.
12 rows: ES, 5 g st, 151 St st, 5 g st, ES.
22 rows: ES, 5 g st, 14 St st, *16 st WM, 11 St st,
rep from * 4 times, 16 st WM, 13 St st, 5 g st, ES.
12 rows: ES, 5 g st, 151 St st, 5 g st, ES.

Work these 68 rows a total of 3 times.

Back neck edge:
Row 1 ES, 5 g st, 16 st WM, 11 St st, 16 st WM, 11 St
st, 16 st WM, M1, 11 g st, 16 st WM, 11 St st, 16 st
WM, 11 St st, 16 st WM, 5 g st, ES (164 sts).
Rows 2 - 10 ES, 5 g st, 16 st WM, 11 St st, 16 st WM,
11 St st, 16 st WM, 12 g st, 16 st WM, 11 St st, 16 st
WM, 11 St st, 16 st WM, 5 g st, ES.
The back is divided into 2 for the front sections.
Each is knit separately.
Row 11 ES, 5 g st, 16 st WM, 11 St st, 16 st WM, 11
St st, 16 st WM, 5 g st, ES. Join a new skein. ES, 5 g
st, 16 st WM, 11 St st, 16 st WM, 11 St st, 16 st WM,
5 g st, ES.

Front sides (worked parallel)
Each front section has 82 sts and is worked
similarly to the back section. The next 11 rows are
worked as follows: ES, 5 g st, *16 st WM, 11 St st st,
rep from * twice, 16 st WM, 5 g st, ES.

Then work as follows over 68 rows:
12 rows: ES, 5 g st, 70 St st, 5 g st, ES.
22 rows: ES, 5 g st, 14 St st, 16 st WM, 11 St st, 16
st WM, 13 St st, 5 g st, ES.

12 R: 1 RM, 5 M kr, 70 M gr, 5 M kr, 1 RM.
22 R: 1 RM, 5 M kr, 14 M gr, 16 M WiM, 11 M gr, 16 M WiM, 13 M gr, 5 M kr, 1 RM.
12 R: 1 RM, 5 M kr, 70 M gr, 5 M kr, 1 RM.
22 R: 1 RM, 5 M kr, *16 M WiM, 11 M gr, von * 2-mal wdh, 16 M WiM, 5 M kr, 1 RM.
Die oben beschriebenen 68 Reihen insg. 3-mal stricken.

Nun noch 10 R in folgender Einteilung stricken:
1 RM, 5 M kr, 70 M gr, 5 M kr, 1 RM.
Anschließend noch 10 Reihen kr über alle M stricken. Alle M locker abketten.

Fertigstellung
Fäden vernähen und feucht spannen.

12 rows: ES, 5 g st, 70 St st, 5 g st, ES.
22 rows: ES, 5 g st, *16 st WM, 11 St st, rep from * twice, 16 st WM, 5 g st, ES.

Work these 68 rows a total of 3 times.

Work 10 rows as follows: ES, 5 g st, 70 St st, 5 g st, ES.

Work 10 rows in g st. Bind off loosely.

Finishing
Weave in ends. Wet block.

Strickschrift: Windmühlenmuster (WiM) / Chart: windmill (WM)

Chart rows (from top to bottom, row numbers on right): 21, 19, 17, 15, 13, 11, 9, 7, 5, 3, 1

	re M / k
o	U / yo
/	2 Mrezus / k2tog
\	ÜZA / skp
3 — 3	3 M rz / C6B
3 — 3	3 M lz / C6F

baxa

Ein der Länge nach gestrickter, sehr leichter und warmer Alpaka/Seidenschal. Das Muster besteht aus einfachen Zöpfen, die von einem Lochmuster unterbrochen werden.

A wide lightweight extra-warm alpaca/silk scarf with a simple cable and openwork pattern. Worked back and forth along the long edge.

Endgröße 165 x 41cm.

Material Claire, 5 Knäuel Fb. 1810 Royal Blue
Maschenmarkierer.

Nadeln Rundstricknadel 5 und 6 mm, 150 cm
lang, Zopfnadel.

Maschenprobe 20 M x 26 R = 10 x 10 cm im
Muster und 5 mm Nadeln.

Muster
Zopfmuster (ZM) (teilbar durch 12 M)
R 1, 3, 5, 7, 11, 13 und 15: alle M re.
Alle geraden R alle M li.
R 9: 6 M auf Hilfsnadel heben und vor die
Arbeit legen, 6 M re, dann die 6 M von der
Hilfsnadel re abstricken.
Reihen 1 – 16 wdh.

Lochmuster (LM) (teilbar durch 2 M)
R 1: *2 Mrezus, U, von * wdh.
R 2 und 4: alle M und U li.
R 3: * U, 2 Mreverzus, von * wdh.
Reihen 1 – 4 wdh.

Anleitung
Mit der 6 mm Nadel 324 M anschlagen. Dann
auf die 5 mm Nadel wechseln und 8 R kr
stricken. Anschließend die Maschen wie folgt
einteilen:
6 M kr, * 6 M LM, 12 M ZM, von * 16-mal wdh, 6
M LM, 6 M kr.
So lange in dieser Einteilung stricken, bis das
Zopfmuster sich 6-mal wiederholt hat (enden
mit der 16. Musterreihe). Dann noch 8 R kr stricken und mit der 6 mm Nadel alle M abketten.

Fertigstellung
Fäden vernähen und feucht spannen.

Measurements 165 x 41 cm (65 x 16").

Yarn *Claire*, 5 skeins #1810 Royal Blue.

Notions cable needle, stitch markers.

Needles 5 and 6 mm: circular 100 cm (40").

Gauge 20 sts and 26 rows = 10 cm (4") in cable
and openwork pattern using 5 mm needle.

Stitches
Cable pattern (CP) (worked over 12 sts).
Rows 1, 3, 5, 7, 11, 13 and 15 knit.
Row 2 and all even rows purl.
Row 9 place 6 sts on cable needle and place in
front of work, k 6 sts, k 6 sts from cable needle.
Repeat rows 1 - 16 for pattern.

Openwork pattern (OP) (worked over 2 sts).
Row 1 *k2tog, yo, rep from *.
Row 2 and all even rows purl.
Row 3 *yo, ssk, rep from *.
Repeat rows 1 - 4 for pattern.

Instructions
With 6 mm needles, cast on 324 sts. Switch to
5 mm needles and work 8 rows in garter st. Set
up pattern as follows: 6 g st, *OP 3 times, CP,
rep from * 16 times, OP 3 times, 6 g st.
Continue as established until the cable pattern
has been knit a total of 6 times ending with
row 16. Work 8 rows in g st. Bind off with 6 mm
needles.

Finishing
Weave in ends and block if necessary.

sinine

Der Umhang wird von unten nach oben mit zwei Fäden gleichzeitig gestrickt. Um das Rechteck in Form zu bringen, wurden entlang des Halsausschnitts mehrere Fältchen eingearbeitet. So entsteht ein zartes, ganz leichtes und elegantes Cape.

The capelet is knit as a rectangle from the bottom up holding two strands of yarn together. Pleats gently pull the capelet together at the neck edge, resulting in a delicate, soft and elegant garment.

Shio ITO 480m (524yd) / 40g
100% Wolle
100% wool

Endgröße Länge: unterer Rand ca. 157 cm, Halsausschnitt ca. 71 cm, Höhe ca. 43 cm.

Material Shio, je 2 Konen Fb. 450 Denim (**A**), Fb. 441 Silver (**B**)
Bei Verwendung nur einer Farbe sind drei Konen ausreichend.
Maschenmarkierer, Knopf (ca 2 cm).

Nadeln Rundstricknadeln 3 und 4,5 mm, mind. 120 cm lang und Nadelspiel 3 mm.

Maschenprobe 22 M x 28 R = 10 x 10 cm in gr mit 4,5 mm Nadeln und mit 2 Fäden gleichzeitig.

Muster

Reliefmuster (ReM): (teilbar durch 10 M)
R 1: 1 M li, 8 M re, 1 M li.
alle geraden R: M stricken, wie sie erscheinen.
R 3: 1 M re, 8 M li, 1 M re.
R 5, 7 und 9: 1 M re, 2 M li, 4 M re, 2 M li, 1 M re.
R 11: wie R 3.
Reihen 1 – 12 wdh.

Rechte Falte (RF) über 15 M:
5 M auf Hilfsnadel 1 abheben. Weitere 5 M auf Hilfsnadel 2 abheben. Nun die 1. Hilfsnadel um 180° nach hinten klappen, so dass die Rückseiten von Hilfsnadel 1 und 2 aufeinander liegen. Nun beide Hilfsnadeln gleichzeitig um 180° nach vorne klappen. Nun sind die 3 Nadeln folgendermaßen angeordnen:
Hilfsnadel 1, Hilfsnadel 2 und Rundstricknadel. Die drei Nadeln liegen parallel und das Gestrick bildet ein Z.
Nun werden die ersten M jeder Nadel zusammen abgestrickt. Dies noch 4-mal wdh, so dass nun aus 15 M noch 5 M erhalten bleiben.

Measurements bottom edge 157 cm (62"), neck edge 71 cm (28"), length 43 cm (17").

Yarn *Shio*, #450 Denim (**A**), #441 Silver (**B**); 2 cones each. If you will only be using one color, then a total of three cones is sufficient.

Needles 3 and 4.5 mm: circular 120 cm (48"); 3mm: two double-pointed.

Notions stitch markers, button 2 cm (3/4").

Gauge 22 sts and 28 rows = 10 cm (4") in St st holding two strands of *Shio* together and 4.5 mm needles.

Stitches

Square pattern (SP) (multiple of 10 sts)
Rows 1, 4 & 12 * p1, k8, p1, rep from *.
Rows 2, 3 & 11 *k1, p8, k1, rep from *.
Rows 5, 7 & 9 *k1, p2, k4, p2, k1, rep from *.
Rows 6, 8 & 10 *p1, k2, p4, k2, p1, rep from *.
Repeat rows 1 - 12 for pattern.

Right pleat (RP) (worked over 15 sts)
Place 5 sts purlwise on a dp needle (Needle A). Place next 5 sts purlwise on another dp needle (Needle B). The two dp needles and the circular needle must now be arranged to form two folds in the fabric. Rotate Needle A so that it is parallel to Needle B and the wrong sides are together. Now rotate Needles A and B together to the **front** of the work. You will have three needles parallel and behind each other, the fabric will look like a Z and needle A is closest to you. *Insert another needle into the first stitch on Needle A, Needle B and the circular needle and knit these together. Repeat from * four times. Reduction of 10 sts.

Linke Falte (LF) über 15 M:
5 M auf Hilfsnadel 1 abheben. Weitere 5 M auf Hilfsnadel 2 abheben. Nun die 1. Hilfsnadel um 180° nach vorne klappen, so dass die Vorderseiten von Hilfsnadel 1 und 2 aufeinander liegen. Nun beide Hilfsnadeln gleichzeitig um 180° nach hinten klappen. Nun sind die 3 Nadeln folgendermaßen angeordnet:
Rundstricknadel, Hilfsnadel 2 und Hilfsnadel 1. Die drei Nadeln liegen parallel und das Gestrick bildet ein S.
Nun werden die ersten M jeder Nadel zusammen abgestrickt. Dies noch 4-mal wdh, so dass nun aus 15 M noch 5 M erhalten bleiben.

Anleitung
Auf der 4,5 mm Rundstricknadel mit je einem Faden in **A** und **B** zusammen 342 M anschlagen.
3 R kr stricken und dann die Maschen wie folgt einteilen:
1 RM, 34-mal ReM, 1 RM.
Nach einem Höhenrapport (= 12 R) Maschen wie folgt einteilen:
1 RM, 1 ReM, 320 M gr, 1 ReM, 1 RM.
In dieser Einteilung stricken, bis der Umhang ca. 37 cm hoch ist (entspricht 8 Höhenrapporten des ReM). Dabei die letzte Reihe (12. Reihe ReM) schon mit der 3 mm Rundstricknadel stricken und dabei bleiben.

Nun die Faltenreihe wie folgt stricken:
1 RM, 1 ReM, *5 M re, LF, von * 7-mal wdh, **RF, 5 M re, von ** 7-mal wdh, 1 ReM, 1 RM (182 M)

Alternative ohne Falten:
1 RM, 1 ReM, *2 Mrezus, von * 159-mal wdh, 1 ReM, 1 RM (182 M).

Für den Halsausschnitt noch 2 R kr, dabei am Ende der zweiten R 10 M anschlingen.
Dann Maschen wie folgt einteilen:
1 RM, 19-mal ReM (ab 4. Reihe), 1 RM.

Left pleat (LP) (worked over 15 sts)
Place 5 sts purlwise on a dp needle (Needle A). Place next 5 sts purlwise on another dp needle (Needle B). The two dp needles and the circular needle must now be arranged to form two folds in the fabric. Rotate Needle A so that it is parallel to Needle B and the right sides are together. Now rotate Needles A and B together to the **back** of the work. You will have three needles parallel and behind each other, the fabric will look like an S and the circular needle is closest to you. *Insert another needle into the first stitch on the circular needle, Needle B, and Needle A and knit these together. Repeat from * four times. Reduction of 10 sts.

Instructions
Cast on 342 sts holding one strand each of **A** and **B** together and using 4.5 mm needles. Knit 3 rows. Begin pattern as follows: ES, SP 34 times, ES. Continue in pattern. After 12 rows, work as follows: ES, SP, 320 St st, SP, ES.

Work until piece measures approx. 37 cm (14.5") from the beginning (8 row repeats of SP or 96 rows in pattern). **For the last row, switch to 3 mm needles.**

Work pleat row with 3 mm needle as follows: ES, SP, *k5, LP, rep from * 7 more times, **RP, k5, rep from ** 7 more times, SP, ES (182 sts).

Alternative If you don't want to make pleats, work the row as follows: ES, SP, *k2tog, rep from * 159 times, SP, ES (182 sts).

Knit two rows and cast on 10 stitches at the end of the second row for the buttonhole flap.
Continue as follows (WS): ES, SP 19 times (this will be Row 4), ES.
AT THE SAME TIME, in Row 9 of SP, add buttonhole. Work in pattern until the last SP repeat (in the

Knopfloch in der 9. R des Reliefmusters wie folgt arbeiten:
am Ende der Reihe im letzten Reliefmuster Rapport, 1 M re, 2 M li, 1 M re, 3 M abk, im Muster weiter stricken.
In der nächsten R an der Abkettstelle 3 M neu anschlingen.
Bis R 12 in ReM weiterstricken. Nochmals R 1 und 2 vom ReM stricken.
1 R re und anschließend abketten.

Fertigstellung
Alle Fäden vernähen und feucht spannen. Knopf annähen.

buttonhole flap). Then k1, p2, k1, bind off 3 sts, continue as established to end.
In the next row, cast on 3 sts where the 3 sts were bound off.
Work through Row 12 in the SP. Work Rows 1 and 2 again. Knit one row. Bind off.

Finishing
Weave in ends. Wet block. Sew on button.

modra

Das Modell wird zunächst als langer Schal gestrickt. Nach dem Spannen wird er so zusammengenäht, dass ein Bolero entsteht. Der Schal enthält verkürzte Reihen und diagonal gestrickte Bereiche. Der Schalbolero kann im Prinzip mit jedem Garn und jedem Muster gestrickt werden. Wichtig ist, dass das Gestrick schön fällt.

The bolero is first knit as a long rectangle incorporating short rows and knitting on the diagonal. After blocking, the rectangle is sewn together to form a bolero. Any yarn can be used to make this bolero — the main criterion is that the knit piece drapes well.

Pearl Lanamania 875m (957yd) / 100g
50% Perlenfaser, 50% Tencel
50% pearl fiber, 50% tencel
Asa ITO 225m (246yd) / 25g
72% Leinen, 18% Baumwolle,10% Seide
72% linen, 18% cotton, 10% silk

Endgröße 30 x 210 cm (gespannt); Kleidergröße 38 - 44. Die Größe des Schalboleros ist einfach zu ermitteln: Die Schalbreite entspricht der halben Rückenlänge und die Schallänge entspricht dem 2-fachen Brustumfang.

Material Pearl, 1 Strang Fb. Midnight (**A**)
Asa, 1 Kone Fb. 52 Blue (**B**).

Nadeln Rundstricknadel 3 mm, 60 cm lang und Häkelnadel 3 mm.

Maschenprobe 30 M x 40 R = 10 x 10 cm in gr und **A**.

Muster
Der gesamte Bolero wird glatt rechts (gr) gestrickt!

Verkürzte Reihen
Das bedeutet, dass eine Reihe nicht vollständig gestrickt wird, sondern zwischendurch die Arbeit gewendet und zurückgestrickt wird. Damit an den Wendestellen keine Löcher entstehen werden sog. **Wendemaschen (WM)** gestrickt. Dabei wird nach dem Wenden die erste Masche mit dem Faden vor der Nadel li abgehoben. Dann wird der Faden fest nach hinten gezogen, so dass eine Doppelmasche entsteht. Diese Doppelmasche wird beim Drüberstricken zusammengestrickt! Aufpassen, dass nicht 2 Maschen daraus gemacht werden. In diesem Modell werden die Reihen immer in 6-er Schritten verkürzt, mal am Ende, mal am Anfang der Reihe.

Verkürzen am Reihenende (VaRE): über 30 R
Alle M im Muster stricken, bis noch 6 M auf der Nadel sind, dann Arbeit wenden, WM arbeiten und alle M zurückstricken.
In der nächsten Reihe wieder alle M im Muster stricken bis noch 12 M auf der Nadel sind,

Measurements 30 x 210 cm (11.8 x 83") - blocked; women's size 38 - 44 (Medium-Large). The size can easily be individualized based on the following measurements: the width is half of your back length and the length is twice your bust size.

Yarn *Pearl*, 1 skein Midnight (**A**)
Asa,1 cone #52 (**B**).

Needles 3mm: circular 60 cm (24") and crochet hook.

Gauge 30 sts and 40 rows = 10 cm (4") in **A** in St st.

Stitches
The entire bolero is worked in St st!

Short rows
When knitting short rows, a row is not knit to the end. Instead, in the middle of a row, the work is turned and worked further. There are many ways to avoid making a hole at the point of turning. In this case, a yarn over method is used.

Short row yarn over (SRYO): wyif slip 1 st purlwise, then move the yarn over the needle and behind the work so that a new stitch is formed (yo). When the entire row is once again worked, this double stitch will be knit together — be careful that they remain together and that an extra stitch isn't formed.
For the bolero, the short rows are worked in 6 st increments — sometimes at the beginning and sometimes at the end of a row.

Short rows at the end of a row (SRER)
(worked over 30 rows)
Work all sts in pattern until 6 sts are left on the needle. Turn the work, make a SRYO and work

Arbeit wenden, WM arbeiten und alle M zurück-stricken.
In der nächsten Reihe alle M entsprechend Muster stricken, bis noch 18 M auf der Nadel sind, Arbeit wenden, WM arbeiten und alle M zurückstricken. In diesem Stil immer in 6-er Schritten weiterarbeiten, bis auch die letzten 6 M verkürzt wurden.

Verkürzen am Reihenanfang (VaRA):
über 30 R
6 M entsprechend Muster stricken, wenden und WM arbeiten, alle M zurückstricken.
In nächster Reihe 12 M im Muster stricken, dabei die WM der Vorreihe zusammenstricken, Arbeit wenden, WM arbeiten und alle M zurückstricken.
In nächster Reihe 18 M im Muster stricken, dabei wieder WM der Vorreihe zusammenstricken, Arbeit wenden, WM arbeiten und alle M zurück-stricken.
In diesem Stil immer in 6-er Schritten weiterarbeiten, bis über alle M gestrickt wurde. Dann noch eine komplette Reihe im Muster über alle M stricken.

Abschnitt 1
Mit **A** 7 R gr (dabei mit RR beginnen), 1 VaRE.
Zu **B** wechseln; 4 R gr.
Zu **A** wechseln; 1 R re, 1 VaRA, 8 R gr, 1 VaRE, 1 R li.

Abschnitt 2
Dazu 4 R mit **B**, 8 R mit **A** und nochmal 4 R mit **B** stricken. Dabei in der 3. und in allen folgenden Hinreihen wie folgt stricken: 1 RM, 1 M re, 1 ÜZA, alle M re bis noch 2 M auf der Nadel sind, 1 M Qzu, 1 M re, 1 RM.
Nun wieder ohne Zu- und Abnahmen in **A**: 1 VaRA, 8 R gr, 1 VaRE.

Abschnitt 3
Mit **B** 4 R gr.
Zu **A** wechseln; 1 R re, 1 VaRA, 8 R gr, 1 VaRE, 1 R li.
Zu **B** wechseln, 4 R gr.

in pattern to the end of the row. In the next row, work until 12 sts are left on the needle, make a SRYO and work in pattern to the end of the row. In the next row, work until 18 sts are left on the needle, make a SRYO and work in pattern to the end of the row. Continue in this manner in 6 st increments until the last 6 sts on the needle are worked.

Short rows at the beginning of a row (SRBR)
(worked over 30 rows)
Work 6 sts in pattern, turn the work, make a SRYO and work in pattern to end. In the next row, work 12 sts in pattern being sure to work the SRYO as one stitch, turn the work, make a SRYO and work in pattern to end. In the next row, work 18 sts in pattern being sure to work the SRYO as one stitch, turn the work, make a SRYO and work in pattern to end. Continue in this manner in 6 st increments until all the stitches in the row have been worked. Then work a complete row in pattern across all stitches.

Section 1 (S1)
Beginning with a WS row, work 7 r in St st in **A**. Work SRER once.
Change to **B**. Beginning with a RS row, work 4 r in St st.
Change to **A** and knit one row. Work SRBR once. Then work 8 r St st and SRER once. Purl one row.

Section 2 (S2)
Work 4 r **B**, 8 r **A** and 4 r **B** in St st. AT THE SAME TIME, in row 3 and all following RS rows work as follows: ES, k1, skp, k until 2 sts left, M1, k1, ES.
Change to **A** and without increases or decreases, work SRBR once, work 8 r in St st and then work SRER once.

Section 3 (S3)
Change to **B** and work 4 r in St st.

Zu **A** wechseln; 1 VaRA, 8 R gr, 1 VaRE.

Abschnitt 4
Dazu 4 R mit **B**, 8 R mit **A** und nochmal 4 R mit **B** stricken. Dabei in der 3. und in allen folgenden Hinreihen wie folgt stricken: 1 RM, 1 M re, 1 M Qzu, alle M re bis noch 4 M auf der Nadel sind, 2 Mrezus, 1 M re, 1 RM.
Ab jetzt wieder ohne Zu- und Abnahme in **A**; 1 R re, 1 VaRA, 8 R gr, 1 VaRE, 1 R li.
Zu **B** wechseln; 4 R gr.
Zu **A** wechseln; 1 VaRa, 1 R re.

Anleitung
90 M mit **A** anschlagen (optional auch als offener Anschlag, siehe unten).
Nun die einzelnen Abschnitte in folgender Reihenfolge stricken:
1, 2, 3, 4, 1, 2, 4, 1, 2, 3, 4
Wenn Sie keinen offenen Anschlag gemacht haben, werden nun alle M locker abgekettet.

Fertigstellung
Der Schal wird in der Mitte gefaltet und der Anfang und das Ende zusammengenäht (ist nun ein großer Loop). Wenn Sie einen offenen Anschlag gearbeitet haben, die M am Ende nicht abketten, sondern dann im Maschenstich zusammennähen. Nun den Schal gut spannen und die Ränder glatt streichen.

Nun wird der „Loop" so hingelegt, dass die Naht in der Mitte ist und an einem Rand die **B** Streifen genau aufeinandertreffen. Genau an diesem Rand den Loop jeweils rechts und links der Naht 15 cm zusammennähen.

Nun noch beide Armlöcher und den gesamten anderen Rand mit einer Runde fester Maschen in **A** umhäkeln. Alle Fäden vernähen.

Change to **A** and k one row. Work SRBR once, 8 r St st, SRER once and p one row.
Change to **B** and work 4 r in St st.
Change to **A**, work SRBR once, work 8 r in St st and then SRER once.

Section 4 (S4)
Work 4 r **B**, 8 r **A** and 4 r **B** in St st. AT THE SAME TIME, in row 3 and all following RS rows work as follows: ES, k1, M1, k until 4 sts left, k2tog, k1, ES.
Change to **A** and without increases or decreases k one row. Work SRBR once, 8 r in St st, SRER once and p one row.
Change to **B** and work 4 r in St st.
Change to **A** and work SRBR once. K one row.

Instructions
With **A**, cast on 90 sts (*optional: provisional cast on*). Work the sections in the following sequence:
S1, S2, S3, S4, S1, S2, S4, S1, S2, S3, S4.
If you did not start with a provisional cast on, then bind off all sts loosely.

Finishing
Sew the cast on and bind off edges together to form a large loop. If you used a provisional cast on, then use a Kitchener stitch to sew the two ends together. Wet block making sure the edges are flat.

The loop should be laid out so that the seam is in the middle and the stripes made by **B** meet along one edge. Sew together along this edge about 15 cm (6") to the right and left of the seam (see Diagram.

With a crochet hook and **A**, work around both armholes and all edges with one row of chain stitch. Weave in ends.

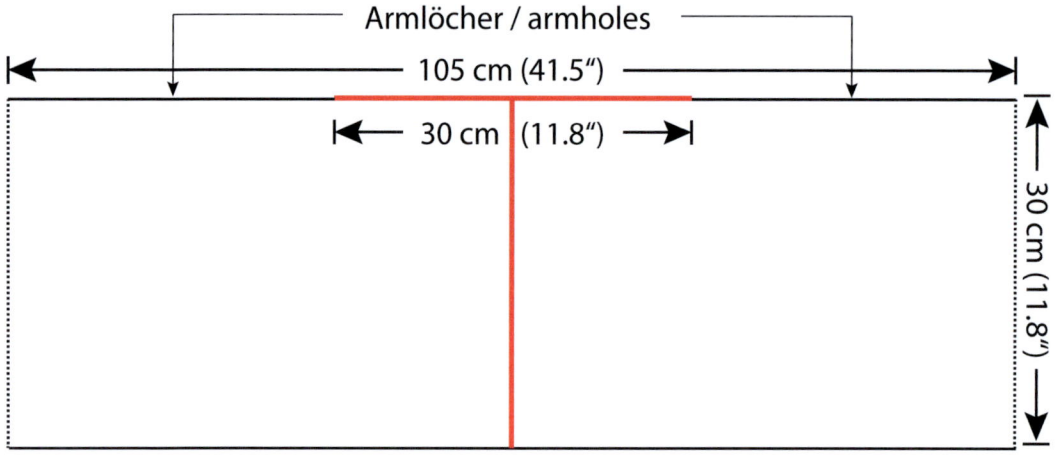

Armlöcher / armholes

105 cm (41.5")

30 cm (11.8")

30 cm (11.8")

——— Naht / seam

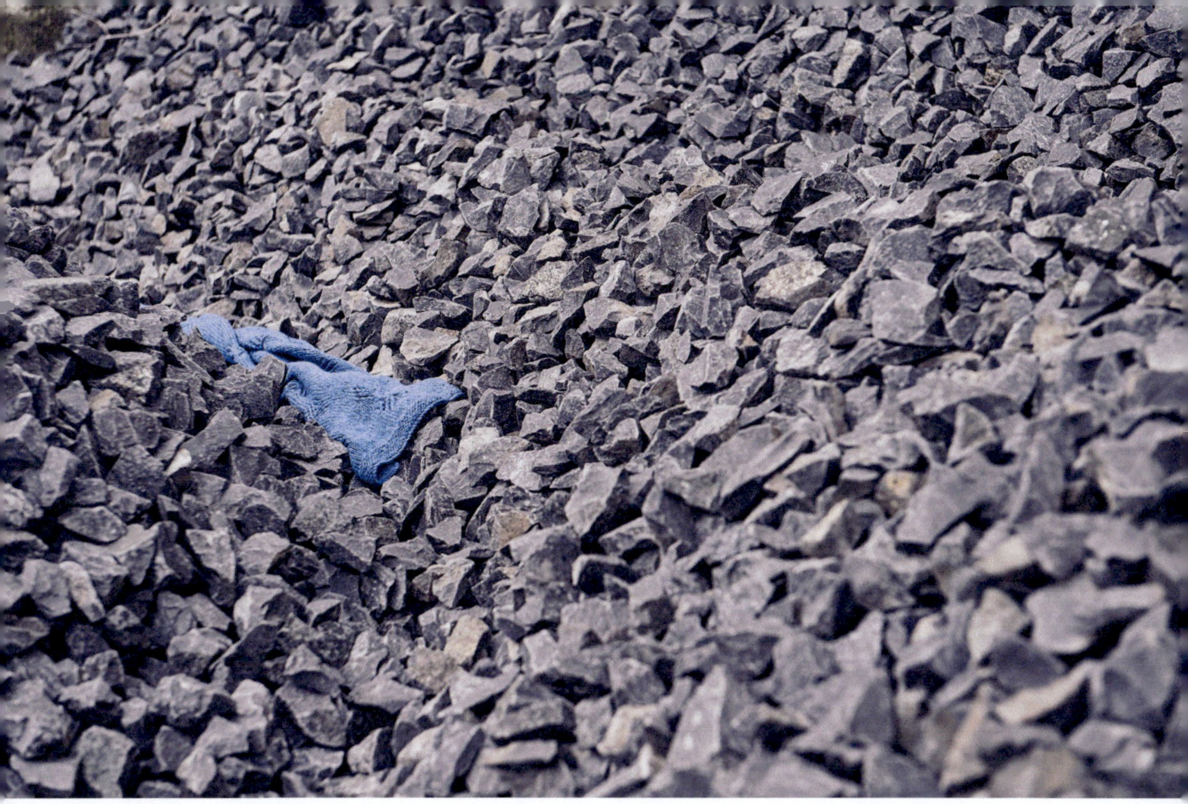

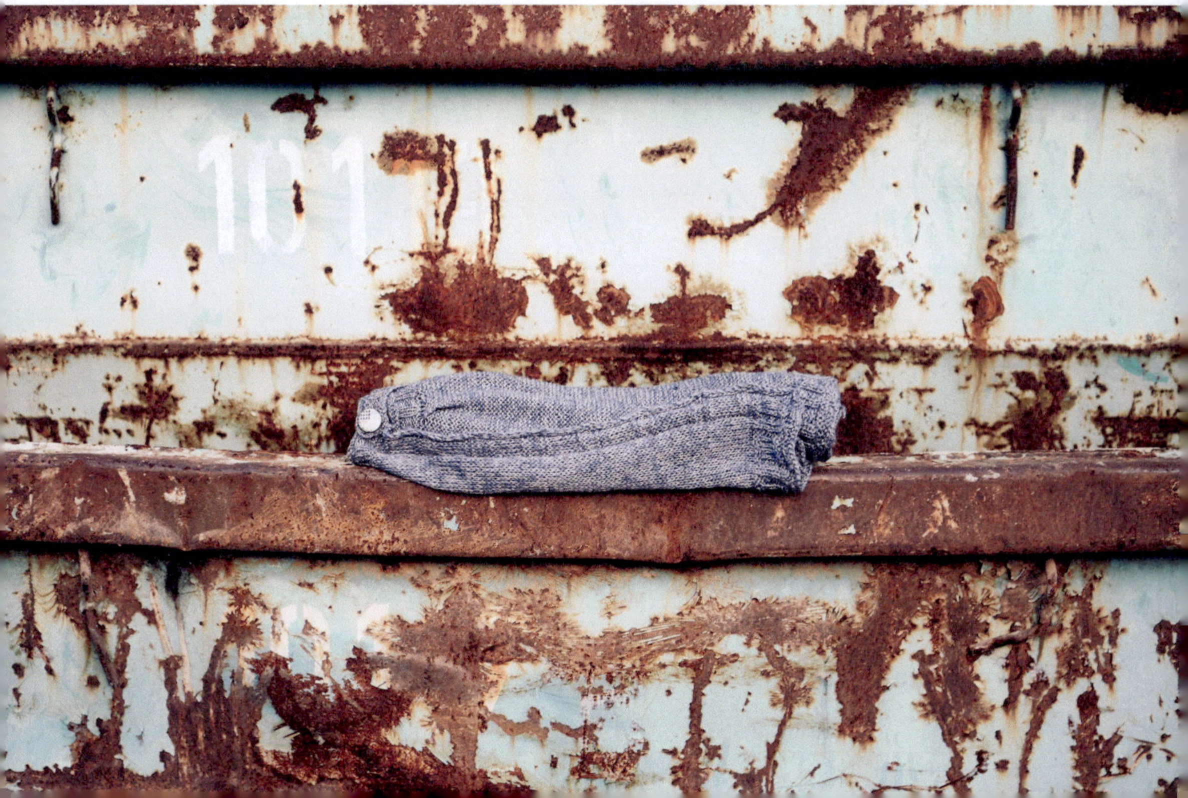
101

uliuli

Ein löchriges, großes Rechteck, welches durch schmale Streifen in kraus rechts durchbrochen wird. Abhängig von der Höhe des Rechtecks ergeben sich verschiedene Tragemöglichkeiten – Schal, Stola oder halber Pareo (hier abgebildet). Das Papiergarn verhält sich nach dem Waschen und Spannen ähnlich wie Seide. Kneten macht es noch weicher.

A large rectangle with an overall lacy pattern is interrupted by colored stripes worked in garter stitch. The width of the rectangle determines its function - scarf, shawl or half-pareo (shown). The paper yarn is similar to silk - after washing and blocking, be sure to knead it to soften.

Washi ITO 250m (373yd) / 25g
54% Papier, 46% Viskose
54% paper, 46% viscose

Endgröße Länge: 152 cm; Höhen: für Schal: 35,5 cm, Stola: 58 cm, halber Pareo: 78 cm

Measurements Length 152 cm (60"); width: scarf - 35.5 cm (14"); shawl - 58 cm (23"); half-pareo - 78 cm (31").

Material Washi, Fb. 266 Aqua (**A**), Fb. 267 Navy (**B**), Fb. 265 Crocus (**C**), Fb. 262 Rainy Day (**D**), Fb. 269 Moss (**E**).
Schal: 2 Konen **A**, je 1 Kone von **B**, **C**, **D** und **E**.
Stola: 3 Konen **A**, je 1 Kone von **B**, **C**, **D** und **E**.
Halber Pareo: 4 Konen **A**, je 1 Kone von **B**, **C**, **D** und **E**.
Maschenmarkierer.

Yarn Washi, #266 Aqua (**A**), #267 Navy (**B**), #265 Crocus (**C**), #262 Rainy Day (**D**), #269 Moss (**E**).
Scarf 2 cones **A**, one cone each **B**, **C**, **D** and **E**.
Shawl 3 cones **A**, one cone each **B**, **C**, **D** and **E**.
Half-pareo 4 cones **A**, one cone each **B**, **C**, **D** and **E**.

Notions Stitch markers.

Nadeln Rundstricknadel 3 mm, 150 cm lang.

Needles 3 mm: circular 150 cm (60").

Maschenprobe: 38 M x 35 R = 10 x 10 cm im Wellenmuster nach dem Spannen.

Gauge 38 sts and 35 rows = 10 cm (4") in wavy pattern after blocking.

Muster
Randmaschen (RM) 1 M li, 1 M re, 1 M li jeweils am Anfang und Ende einer Reihe stricken.

Stitches
Edge stitches (ES) p1, k1, p1 at beginning and end of each row.

Wellenmuster (WM) teilbar durch 24 + 1 M:
R 1: 1 M re, * 4 x 2 Mrezus, 7 x (U, 1 M re), U, 4 x 2 Mreverzus, MS, 1 M re, von * wdh.
R 2: alle M und U li.
Reihen 1 – 2 wdh.

Wavy pattern (WP) (multiple of 24 sts + 1)
Row 1 k1, *k2tog 4 times, (yo, k1) 7 times, yo, ssk 4 times, pm, k1; rep from *.
Row 2 p all sts.
Repeat rows 1-2 for pattern.

Musterabfolge
*8 R WM, 6 R kr, 8 R WM, 4 R kr, von * wdh.

The **row sequence** is always *8 rows wavy pattern (WP), 6 rows garter stitch (g st), 8 rows WP, 4 rows g st. Repeat from *.

Anleitung
Mit **A** 583 M anschlagen. 1 R re, 1 R li und 1 R re stricken. Anschließend die Maschen wie folgt einteilen:
3 Randmaschen, 24 x WM, 3 Randmaschen.
Dann entsprechend der Farb- und Musterabfolge wie unten beschrieben weiterstricken:

Instructions
With **A**, cast on 583 sts. Knit one row. Purl one row. Knit one row.
Establish pattern as follows: 3 ES, WP a total of 24 times, 3 ES. Follow the color and pattern sequence below. For scarf end at *. For shawl end at **. For half-pareo end at ***.

Farb- und Musterabfolge:

8 R WM **A**, 2 R kr **C**, 2 R kr **E**, 2 R kr **A**, 8 R WM **C**, 4 R kr **D**, 8 R WM **B**, 2 R kr **E**, 2 R kr **D**, 2 R kr **B**, 8 R WM **A**, 2 R kr **C**, 2 R kr **E**, 8 R WM **A**, 2 R kr **D**, 2 R kr **B**, 2 R kr **C**, 8 R WM **B**, 2 R kr **E**, 2 R kr **D**, 8 R WM **A**, 2 R kr **C**, 2 R kr **E**, 2 R kr **D**, 8 R WM **A**, 2 R kr **E**, 2 R kr **C**, 8 R WM **A**, * Schal
2 R kr **B**, 2 R kr **D**, 2 R kr **C**, 8 R WM **D**, 2 R kr **B**, 2 R kr **C**, 8 R WM **A**, 2 R kr **B**, 2 R kr **C**, 2 R kr **E**, 8 R WM **A**, 2 R kr **D**, 2 R kr **B**, 8 R WM **C**, 2 R kr **E**, 2 R kr **A**, 2 R kr **D**, 8 R WM **A**, ** Stola
2 R kr **C**, 2 R kr **D**, 8 R WM **B**, 2 R kr **A**, 2 R kr **B**, 2 R kr **E**, 8 R WM **A**, 2 R kr **E**, 2 R kr **A**, 8 R WM **B**, 2 R kr **D**, 2 R kr **A**, 2 R kr **C**, 8 R WM **A**, 2 R kr **B**, 2 R kr **E**, 8 R WM **A** *** halber Pareo

Nach gewünschtem Model in **A** jeweils noch 1 R li, 1 R re, 1 R li stricken. Dann alle M locker abketten.

Fertigstellung
Fäden vernähen und feucht spannen.

Color Sequence in Pattern:

8 r WP **A**, 2 r g st **C**, 2 r g st **E**, 2 r g st **A**, 8 r WP **C**, 4 r g st **D**, 8 r WP **B**, 2 r g st **E**, 2 r g st **D**, 2 r g st **B**, 8 r WP **A**, 2 r g st **C**, 2 r g st **E**, 8 r WP **A**, 2 r g st **D**, 2 r g st **B**, 2 r g st **C**, 8 r WP **B**, 2 r g st **E**, 2 r g st **D**, 8 r WP **A**, 2 r g st **C**, 2 r g st **E**, 2 r g st **D**, 8 r WP **A**, 2 r g st **E**, 2 r g st **C**, 8 r WP **A**, *
2 r g st **B**, 2 r g st **D**, 2 r g st **C**, 8 r WP **D**, 2 r g st **B**, 2 r g st **C**, 8 r WP **A**, 2 r g st **B**, 2 r g st **C**, 2 r g st **E**, 8 r WP **A**, 2 r g st **D**, 2 r g st **B**, 8 r WP **C**, 2 r g st **E**, 2 r g st **A**, 2 r g st **D**, 8 r WP **A**, **
2 r g st **C**, 2 r g st **D**, 8 r WP **B**, 2 r g st **A**, 2 r g st **B**, 2 r g st **E**, 8 r WP **A**, 2 r g st **E**, 2 r g st **A**, 8 r g st **B**, 2 r g st **D**, 2 r g st **A**, 2 r g st **C**, 8 r WP **A**, 2 r g st **B**, 2 r g st **E**, 8 r WP **A** ***.

In **A**, purl one row, knit one row, purl one row. Bind off loosely.

Finishing
Weave in ends. Wet block.

albastru

Die Decke besteht aus 25 kraus rechts und diagonal gestrickten Einzelteilen — 9 großen und 4 kleinen Quadraten sowie 12 Rechtecken. Nach dem Zusammennähen der Einzelteile wird der äußere Rand in 4 Teilen angestrickt und seine Ecken anschließend zusammengenäht.

The baby blanket is knit in garter stitch on the diagonal as 25 separate pieces — 9 large squares, 12 rectangles and 4 small squares. After the pieces have been sewn together, the outer band is picked up and knit in 4 sections and the corners are then sewn together.

Baby Cashmerino Debbie Bliss 125m (136yd) / 50g
50% Wolle, 33% Polyacryl, 12% Kaschmir
50% wool, 33% acrylic, 12% cashmere

Endgröße 81 x 81 cm.

Material Baby Cashmerino, 4 Knäuel Fb. 59 (**A**), 4 Knäuel Fb. 89 (**B**) und 3 Knäuel Fb. 202 (**C**).

Nadeln Rundstricknadel 3 mm, 60 und 100 cm lang.

Maschenprobe 24 M x 48 R = 10 x 10 cm in kr.

Grundmuster kraus rechts (kr).

Diagonalmuster
Die erste M wird immer rechts abgehoben (1 M reabh).
Zunahmereihe (jede Reihe gleich)
1 M reabh, alle M re bis noch 2 M übrig sind, 1 M verd, 1 M re.
Abnahmereihe (jede Reihe gleich)
1 M reabh, 2 Mrezus, restliche M re.

Anleitung
Großes Quadrat (9-mal)
Farbabfolge: *4 R **B**, 8 R **C**, 4 R **B**, 8 R **A**, von * wdh.
Mit **B** 3 M anschlagen und ab sofort nur kr stricken.
R 1: 1 M reabh, 1 M verd, 1 M re.
R 2: 1 M reabh, 1 M re, 1 M verd, 1 M re.
R 3: 1 M reabh, 2 M re, 1 M verd, 1 M re (6 M insg).
Zu **C** wechseln und in der oben beschriebenen Farbabfolge gemäß den Zunahmereihen so lange stricken, bis insg. 76 M auf der Nadel sind (sollte nach 2 R in **B** sein). Nun wieder in der Farbabfolge bleiben, aber diesmal gemäß der Abnahmereihen stricken, bis nur noch 3 M auf der Nadel sind. Diese dann abketten.

Kleines Quadrat (4-mal)
Mit **C** 3 M anschlagen. So lange gemäß Zunahmereihen stricken, bis 10 M auf der Nadel sind. Dann gemäß Abnahmereihen stricken bis nur noch 3 M auf der Nadel sind. Faden abschneiden, durch die

Measurements 81 x 81 cm (32").

Yarn *Baby Cashmerino*, 4 skeins #59 (**A**), 4 skeins #89 (**B**) and 3 skeins #202 (**C**).

Needles 3 mm: circular 60 and 100 cm (24 and 40").

Gauge 24 sts and 48 rows = 10 cm (4") in g st.

Basic pattern garter stitch.

Diagonal pattern
The first stitch is always slipped **knitwise** (sl 1).

Increase row (worked every row)
sl 1, knit until 2 sts remain, kfb, k1.

Decrease row (worked every row)
sl 1, k2tog, k to end.

Instructions
Large square (make 9)
The color sequence is as follows: *4 r **B**, 8 r **C**, 4 r **B**, 8 r **A**, rep from *.
With **B**, cast on 3 sts.
Next row: sl 1, kfb, k1.
Next row: sl 1, k1, kfb, k1.
Next row: sl 1, k2, kfb, k1 (6 sts).
Change to **C** and continue working increase rows and AT THE SAME TIME maintaining the color sequence until there are 76 sts. This should be after knitting two rows of **B**. Maintain color sequence and begin decrease rows. Work until 3 sts remain. Bind off 3 sts.

Small square (make 4)
With **C**, cast on 3 sts. Work increase row until there are 10 sts. Work decrease row until 3 sts remain. Pull thread through last 3 sts and pull tight.

3 Maschen fädeln und festziehen.

Rechtecke (12-mal)

Mit **B** 3 M anschlagen und gemäß Zunahmereihen solange stricken, bis 10 M auf der Nadel sind. Anschließend die beiden folgenden Reihen so lange wiederholen, bis das Rechteck an der langen Seite 23 cm misst:

R 1: 1 M reabh, 2 Mrezus, alle M re bis noch 2 M auf der Nadel sind, 1 M verd, 1 M re.

R 2: 1 M reabh, restliche M re.

Nun gemäß den Abnahmereihen so lange stricken, bis nur noch 3 M auf der Nadel sind. Faden abschneiden, durch die 3 Maschen fädeln und festziehen.

Fertigstellung

Alle Teile gut in Form ziehen und entsprechend dem Diagramm auslegen. Sorgen Sie dafür, dass die Diagonalen des inneren Rahmens (kleine Quadrate und Rechtecke) in die gleiche Richtung laufen und die Anfangs- und Endfäden immer am gleichen Punkt sind. Der Gesamteindruck wird von der Richtung der Diagonalen der großen Quadrate bestimmt. Sie können alle in die gleiche Richtung zeigen oder aber variieren. Falls sie rotieren, achten Sie darauf, dass die Farben an den Schnittpunkten übereinstimmen.

Das Zusammennähen braucht ein bisschen Geduld. Es ist wichtig, die Stiche sauber und eher locker zu machen, damit die Nähte nicht hart werden und die Decke schön fällt. Es ist einfacher, wenn zuerst der Innenrahmen zusammengenäht wird und anschließend die großen Quadrate eingesetzt werden.

Äußerer Rand

Mit **A** entlang einer Kante 178 M aufnehmen und 12 R kr stricken (mit HR enden). Gleichzeitig für die Eckzunahmen an beiden Enden in den Hinrei-

Rectangle (make 12)

With **B**, cast on 3 sts. Work increase rows until there are 10 sts. Then work the following 2 row sequence until the rectangle is 23 cm (9") long:

Row 1 sl 1, k 2tog, knit until 2 sts remain, kfb, k1.

Row 2 sl 1, k to end of row.

Work decrease row until 3 sts remain. Pull thread through last 3 sts and pull tight.

Finishing

Pull and tug the squares and rectangles into shape. Lay all 25 pieces out on a large surface according to the diagram. Make sure the g st row diagonals for the frame (rectangles and small squares) are all in the same direction and that your starting and end tails are also in the same spot on each piece. The overall look will depend on the rotation of the large striped squares. The stripes can be in the same direction or varied. If rotating the squares, be sure that the stripes match at the edges for a nicer look.

Sewing together the pieces is an exercise in patience. It is important to keep the stitching neat and relatively loose so that there are no tight seams and the blanket drapes. Use the edge stitches and work a loose whip stitch when sewing. It is easier to first sew the frame together (small squares and rectangles) and then ease the larger squares within the frame.

Outer edge

With the right side facing and using **A**, pick up and knit 178 sts along one edge. Work in g st a total of 12 rows ending with a RS row. AT THE SAME

hen je 1 M zunehmen. In der RR alle M abketten. Mit den anderen 3 Kanten gleich verfahren und anschließend die Ecken zusammennähen.

Alle Fäden vernähen. Nass spannen.

TIME, increase one stitch at each end on every RS row. Bind off (WS). Do the same for the other 3 edges. Sew seams at corners.

Weave in ends. Wet block.

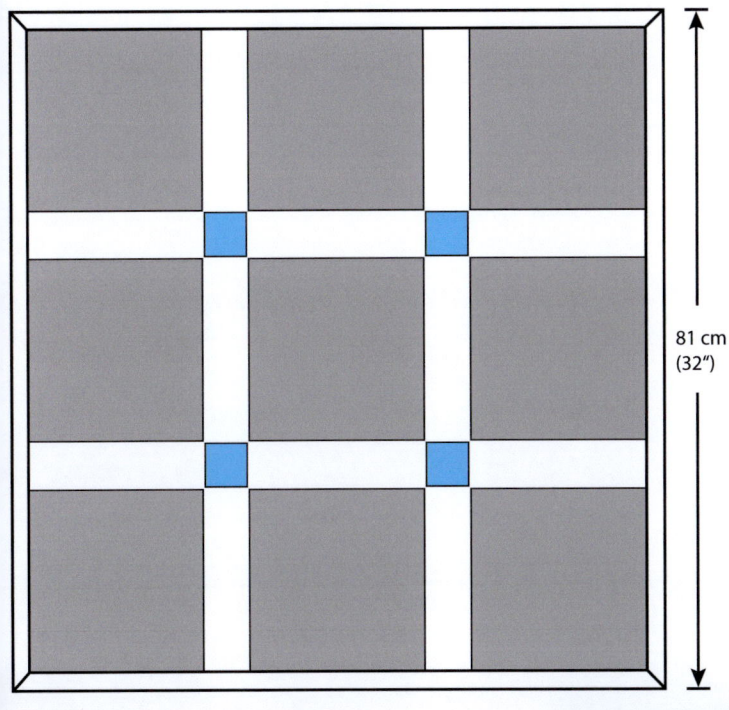

81 cm
(32")

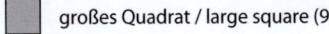 großes Quadrat / large square (9)

 kleines Quadrat / small square (4)

Rechtecke / rectangles (12)

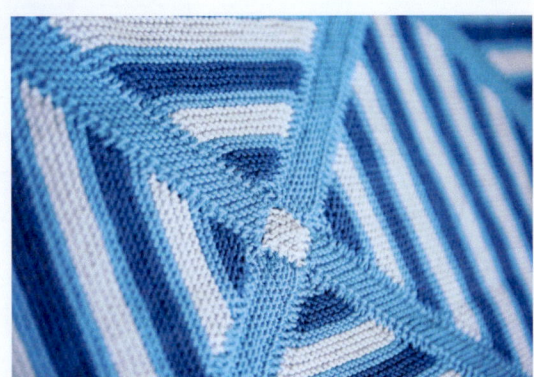

luhlaza

Das Kissen wird als langes Rechteck gestrickt, anschließend gefaltet und an den Seiten zusammengenäht. Es werden 4 unterschiedliche Hebemaschen verwendet. Ja, auch das 2-farbige Ornamentenmuster wurde mit Hebemaschen erstellt.

The pillow is knit as a long rectangle and then folded and sewn together. Four different slip stitches are used — including the two-color pattern.

Endgröße 40 x 40 cm.

Material Rialto 4-ply, 4 Knäuel Fb. 13 (**A**), 1 Knäuel Fb. 37 (**B**).
Maschenmarkierer.
40 cm x 40 cm Kissen.

Nadeln Rundstricknadel 3 mm, 60 cm lang.

Maschenprobe 30 M x 58 R = 10 x 10 cm im versetzten Hebemaschenmuster (VHM).

Muster
2/2 Rippenmuster (gerade Maschenzahl)
R 1: *2 M re, 2 M li; von * wdh, 2 M re.
R 2: Maschen stricken, wie sie erscheinen.
Reihen 1 und 2 wdh.

Alle Hebemaschen werden li abgehoben.
Basishebemasche (BHM):
(teilbar durch 2 + 2 M)
R 1: *1 M re, 1 M abh, von * wdh, 2 M re.
R 2: alle M li.
Reihen 1 und 2 wdh.

Versetzte Hebemasche (VHM):
(teilbar durch 2 + 2 M)
R 1: *1 M re, 1 M abh, von * wdh, 2 M re.
Alle geraden R: alle M li.
R 3: 2 M re, *1 M abh, 1 M re, von * wdh.
Reihen 1 – 4 wdh.

Doppelt versetzte Hebemasche (DVHM):
(teilbar durch 2 + 2 M)
R 1 + 3: *1 M re, 1 M abh, von * wdh, 2 M re.
Alle geraden R alle M li.
R 5 + 7: 2 M re, *1 M abh, 1 M re, von * wdh.
Reihen 1 – 8 wdh.

2-Farben Hebemaschen (2FHM)
(siehe Diagramm)
1. Die Farben wechseln alle 2 Reihen – die

Measurements 40 x 40 cm (15.75").

Yarn *Rialto 4ply*, 4 skeins #13 (**A**), 1 skein #37 (**B**).

Notions 40 cm square pillow, stitch markers.

Needles 3 mm: circular 60 cm (24").

Gauge 30 sts and 58 rows = 10 cm (4") in shifted slip stitch (SSS) pattern.

Stitches
2/2 Rib (even number of stitches)
Row 1 *k2, p2, rep from *, k2.
Row 2 *p2, k2, rep from *, p2.
Repeat rows 1 and 2.

Slip all stitches as if to **purl**.
Basic slip stitch (BSS) (multiple of 2 sts plus 2)
Row 1 *k1, sl 1, rep from *, k2.
Row 2 purl.
Repeat rows 1 and 2 for pattern.

Shifted slip stitch (SSS)
(multiple of 2 sts plus 2)
Row 1 *k1, sl 1, rep from *, k2.
Row 2 and all even rows purl.
Row 3 k2, *sl 1, k1, rep from *.
Repeat rows 1 - 4 for pattern.

Double shifted slip stitch (DSSS)
(multiple of 2 sts plus 2)
Rows 1 & 3 *k1, sl 1, rep from *, k2.
Row 2 and all even rows purl.
Row 5 & 7 k2, *sl 1, k1, rep from *.
Repeat rows 1 - 8 for pattern.

Slip stitch color pattern (SSCP) - see diagram
1. Colors are alternated every 2 rows — the color next to the row count is the color used

in der Reihenzahl angezeigte Farbe wird für die nächsten beiden Reihen verwendet, z.B. die Reihen 1 und 2 werden in **A** gestrickt, die Reihen 3 und 4 in **B**.

2. In jeder Reihe wird nur mit 1 Farbe gestrickt! Die Maschen in der anderen Farbe werden links abgehoben. Dabei den Faden in den HR hinter der Arbeit und in den RR vor der Arbeit mitführen.

Anleitung

Mit **A** 122 M anschlagen und über 10 Reihen im 2/2 Rippenmuster stricken. Anschließend 1 R re und 1 R li. Nun mit dem VHM-Muster beginnen. Dieses so lange stricken, bis das Strickstück insg. 30 cm lang ist. Nun 2 R stricken. Diese Reihen markieren die erste Falte.

*Zu **B** wechseln und 4 R gr stricken. Anschließend die M folgendermaßen einteilen: RM, 2FHM 4-mal, RM. Nun 46 R entsprechend dem Diagramm im 2FHM-Muster arbeiten, von * 3-mal wdh. Zum Schluss nochmals 4 R gr in **B** stricken.
Wieder zu **A** wechseln und 3 R re stricken (markieren die 2. Falte). 1 R li und anschließend ca. 21,5 cm im DVHM-Muster stricken. Nun 2 R re (markieren die 3. Falte) und anschließend nochmals 3 cm im BHM-Muster stricken. Nun alle M wie folgt abketten: 1 M re, *1 M abh, 1 M abk, 1 M re, 1 M abk, von * wdh.

Fertigstellung

Strickstück spannen. Nun wie folgt zusammennähen: Stück an der 3. Faltlinie nach innen klappen und über die gesamte Breite annähen. Entlang der 1. Faltlinie Stück nach innen klappen und mit dem Matratzenstich die Seiten zusammennähen.
Zu Letzt entlang der 2. Faltlinie Stück ebenfalls nach innen falten (überlappt den anderen Teil) und ebenfalls die Seiten zusammennähen.

for 2 rows, e.g., rows 1 and 2 are worked in **A** and rows 3 and 4 are worked in **B**.
2. In each row, only one color is worked. The stitches of the other color are slipped with the yarn in back on the RS rows and with the yarn in front on the WS rows. For instance, in row 1, sl 2 sts, k 26 sts in **A**, sl 2 sts. In row 2, sl 2 sts, p 26 sts in **A**, sl 2 sts. In row 3, k 2 sts in **B**, sl 2 sts, k22 sts in **B**, sl 2 sts, k 2 sts etc.

Instructions

With **A** cast on 122 sts. Work 10 rows in 2/2 Rib. Knit 1 row. Purl 1 row. Begin SSS pattern. Work until piece measures 30 cm (11.8") from the cast on edge. Knit 2 rows. This will form Fold 1.

*Using **B** work 4 rows in St st. Set up SSCP as follows: ES, SSCP 4 times, ES. Work 46 rows in pattern (see Stitches for important information about how this pattern is worked). Repeat from * 3 more times. Work 4 rows St st in **B**.

Change to **A**. Knit 3 rows - this will form Fold 2. Purl 1 row. Work DSSS pattern until about 21.5 cm (ca 8.5") from Fold 2. Knit 2 rows creating Fold 3. Work BSS pattern for 3 cm (1.2"). Bind off as follows: k1, *sl 1, psso, k1, psso, rep from *.

Finishing

Wet block. Using the folding lines and the sketch as a guideline, sew the pillowcase together in the following sequence: Fold the piece inwards at Fold 3 so that wrong sides are facing and sew the flap down across the entire width. Now fold inwards at Fold 1 and using a mattress stitch sew in place along the side seams. Next fold inwards at Fold 2 (this will produce an overlap) and using a mattress stitch sew the side seam together. Weave in ends.

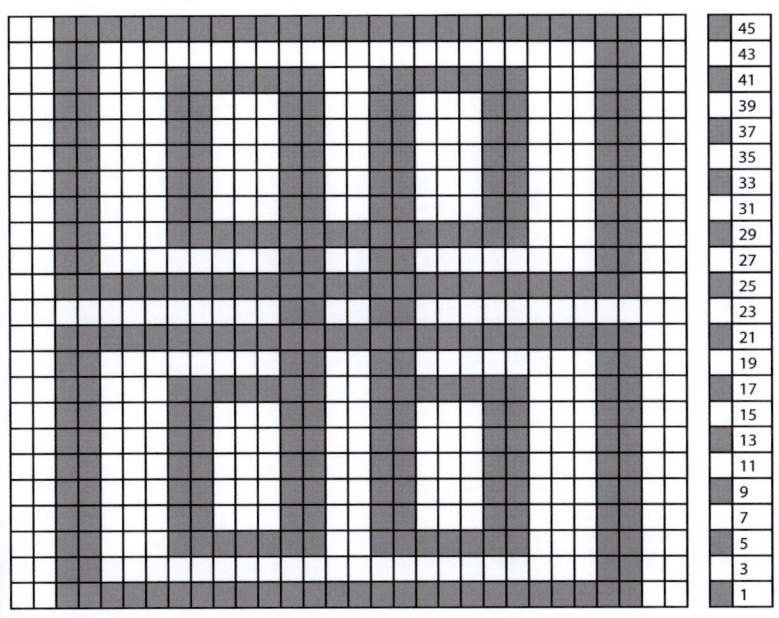

45	
43	
41	
39	
37	
35	
33	
31	
29	
27	
25	
23	
21	
19	
17	
15	
13	
11	
9	
7	
5	
3	
1	

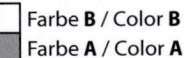 Farbe **B** / Color **B**
Farbe **A** / Color **A**

Diagramm zum 2FHM / chart for SSCP

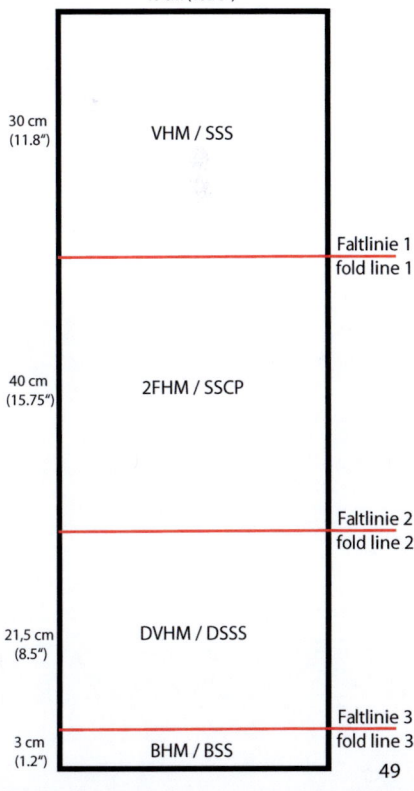

40 cm (15.75")

30 cm
(11.8") — VHM / SSS

Faltlinie 1
fold line 1

40 cm
(15.75") — 2FHM / SSCP

Faltlinie 2
fold line 2

21,5 cm
(8.5") — DVHM / DSSS

Faltlinie 3
fold line 3

3 cm
(1.2") — BHM / BSS

yax

Leichtes und transportables Filzkissen. Aus-gerollt für zwei Personen gedacht, oder in der Mitte gefaltet ist es extra warm für eine Per-son. Zwei Quadrate werden getrennt vonein-ander jeweils von innen nach außen gestrickt. Anschließend werden beide Teile verbunden und ein Verschlussriegel angestrickt. Zusätz-lich kann zum Transport noch eine Kordel hergestellt werden.

Lightweight and transportable felted sitting pad for one or two. Roll out to full length for two or fold in half for extra warmth for one. Two squares are knit separately from the center outwards. The squares are joined and a border is added using a non-felting yarn. The flap is knit on. An optional cord allows you to carry the pad over your shoulder.

Studio Lang Yarns 200m (218yd) / 50g
87% Wolle, 12% Nylon, 1% Elastan
87% wool, 12% nylon, 1% elastane
Rialto 4-ply Debbie Bliss 180m (196yd) / 50g
100% Wolle
100% wool

Endgröße Länge insg. (mit Riegel) nach dem Filzen: 91cm; Breite 32 cm. Jedes Quadrat misst 32 x 32 cm

Material Studio, 2 Knäuel Fb. 33 (**A**), 1 Knäuel Fb. 58 (**B**), 1 Knäuel Fb.94 (**C**).
Rialto 4-ply, 1 Knäuel Fb. 37 (**D**) (es wurden ca. 10g benötigt).
Maschenmarkierer, Druckknöpfe (13 mm), große Sicherheitsnadeln, um Maschen stillzulegen.

Nadeln Rundstricknadel 5 mm, 60 und 100 cm lang, Nadelspiel 5 mm, Rundstricknadel 4 mm, 60 cm lang.

Maschenprobe 18 M x 26 R = 10 x 10 cm gr mit „Studio", 5 mm Nadeln und vor dem Filzen.

Techniken
3 needle bind off (mit 3 Nadeln zusammenstricken und dabei abketten) – Technik die dann angewendet wird, wenn 2 Strickstücke final miteinander verbunden werden. Dazu die beiden Strickstücke mit den Außenseiten aufeinander legen, so dass beide Nadeln in der linken Hand direkt hintereinander liegen. Nun in die erste M der vorderen Nadel und dann in die erste M der hinteren Nadel einstechen, beide zusammenstricken und auf die rechte Nadel heben (nur noch 1 M). Das gleiche mit den nächsten Maschen machen. Nun sind auf der rechten Nadel 2 M, nun 1 M normal abketten. Anschließend wieder 2 M zusammenstricken und dann wieder abketten. So lange wiederholen bis die letzen beiden M zusammengestrickt und abgekettet wurden.

I-Cord (wie Stricklieselkordel) – man benötigt 2 Spielnadeln und es wird immer nur rechts gestrickt! 5 M anschlagen und 1 R re. *Strickstück nicht wenden, sondern auf der Spielnadel wieder nach rechts schieben. Den Faden hinten herum führen und die 5 M wieder rechts abstricken, ab *

Measurements after felting Total length including flap 91 cm (36"); width 32 cm (12.5"). Each square is 32 x 32 cm (12.5" x 12.5").

Yarn Studio, 2 skeins #33 (**A**), 1 skein #58 (**B**), 1 skein #94 (**C**).
Rialto 4-ply, #37 (**D**), 1 skein (approx. 10 g were used).

Notions Stitch markers, snap fasteners 13 mm (1/2"), stitch holders or spare needles.

Needles 5 mm: set of 5 double-pointed (dp); circular 60 and 100 cm (24 and 40").
4 mm: circular 60 cm (24").

Gauge 18 sts and 26 rows = 10 cm (4") in St st using Studio before felting using 5 mm needles.

Techniques
3-needle bind-off is used to join two edges with the same number of stitches, each on a separate needle. Arrange so that the right sides of the pieces are facing, the needles are parallel and in your left hand. Insert a third needle into the first stitch on each needle, knit them together and move the new stitch onto the right needle. Knit the next stitch the same way. Pass the first stitch over the second stitch on the right hand needle. Continue until all the stitches have been worked.

I-cord An I-cord is a long thin tube knit on dp needles. Cast on 5 sts and k 1 row.
*Do not turn. Slide the stitches back to the other end of the needle. With the yarn in back, knit the row again. Repeat from * to desired length. It helps to pull on the tube every now and again to

wdh. Kordel so lange stricken wie gewünscht und am Ende alle M abketten.

Anleitung

Jedes Quadrat wird separat aus der Mitte heraus glatt rechts (gr) gestrickt. Man beginnt mit 8 Maschen und endet mit 320. Wenn genug M vorhanden sind, von den Spielnadeln auf die Rundstricknadel wechseln. In jeder ungeraden Runde werden 8 M zugenommen.

Quadrat 1

Die Farbabfolge ist: 16 R **A**, 8 R **B**, 4 R **C**, 16 R **A**, 8 R **B**, 4 R **C**, 23 R **A**.

8 M in **A** anschlagen und gleichmäßig auf die 4 Spielnadeln verteilen. Runde schließen, dabei aufpassen, dass sich die M nicht verdrehen. Die ersten Reihen sind etwas fummelig, es wird aber besser, je mehr M auf der Nadel sind. 1 R re. In der nächsten R jede M verdoppeln (16 M). 1 R re. Nächste R die erste und letzte M jeder Spielnadel verdoppeln (24 M). 1 R re. In dieser Weise weiterstricken, also jede 2. R die ersten und letzten M jeder Spielnadel verdoppeln.

Wenn die Maschen auf eine Rundstricknadel gestrickt werden, muss ein Maschenmarkierer jeweils am Ende einer Spielnadel gesetzt werden. Die Zunahmen erfolgen dann vor und nach dem Markierer.

Nach 16 R sollten 64 M auf der Nadel sein, dann zu **B** wechseln und nach wie vor jede 2. R 8 M zunehmen. Nun im Farbmuster bis zur 18. R der letzten **A**-Sequenz stricken. Die letzten 5 Runden werden kr gestrickt, was soviel bedeutet, dass die 19., 21. und 23. Runde links gestrickt werden. Dabei jeweils 8 M zunehmen. Alle M stilllegen!

distribute the tension. Work to desired length and bind off.

Instructions

Each square is knit separately in St st starting from the center and working outwards knitting in the round. Begin with 8 sts and work up to 320 sts. Change from dp to circular needles as necessary to accommodate the increased stitch count. Eight stitches are increased every other round (odd rounds) throughout.

Square 1

The color sequence for Square 1 is as follows: 16 r **A**, 8 r **B**, 4 r **C**, 16 r **A**, 8 r **B**, 4 r **C**, 23 r **A**.

Cast on 8 stitches in **A**. Divide the stitches evenly among 4 dp needles. Join round being careful not to twist stitches. Knit one round. In next round, kfb 8 times (16 sts). Knit one round. Kfb in first and last stitch on each dp needle (24 sts). Knit one round. At the beginning, this will be very awkward, but as more stitches are added it becomes easier.

While the stitches are evenly distributed on dp needles, increases are made on the first and last stitch on each needle. When changing to circular needles, place stitch markers at the end of each dp needle — then increase in the stitch before and after the stitch marker in the increase rounds.

After 16 rounds there should be 64 stitches. Switch to **B** and continue increasing 8 stitches every other round for 8 rounds. Switch to **C**. Continue in this manner following the color sequence above.

Note: In the last **A** sequence, work 18 rounds. Continue with **A** and work the last 5 rounds in g st which in the round means that rounds 19, 21 and 23 in the last **A** sequence are purled. Be sure to increase in these purl rounds (odd rounds). Place stitches on a spare needle.

Quadrat 2

Die Farbabfolge ist: *4 R **A**, 4 R **B**, 4 R **A**, 4 R **C**, von * 2-mal wdh, 4 R **A**, 4 R **B**, 23 R **A**.
Wie beim ersten Quadrat arbeiten, nur mit der anderen Farbfolge.

Fertigstellung

Für das Abketten, die Ränder und das Zusammenstricken wird nun zu 4 mm Nadeln und **D** gewechselt. Das wird den Rand unschön zusammenziehen, aber nach dem Filzen ist alles eben und plan.

3 Seiten (240 M) von Quadrat 2 mit 4 mm Nadeln und **D** abketten. Nun über die verbliebenen 80 M noch 5 R gr stricken und Arbeit stilllegen.

Bei Quadrat 1 100 M ebenfalls mit 4 mm Nadeln und **D** abketten. Dann das Garn abschneiden und die folgenden 40 M stilllegen. Wieder die folgenden 100 M wie oben abketten. Nun die verbliebenden 80 M mit den 80 M des Quadrat 2 auf der linken Seite zusammenstricken und gleichzeitig abketten (3 needle bind off).

Der Riegel wird nun kr und mit 5 mm Nadeln und der Filzwolle „Studio" direkt an die 40 stillgelegten M angestrickt. Dazu 24 R **A**, 4 R **C** und 80 R **B** stricken. Am Ende alle M abketten.

Fäden so vernähen, dass evtl. entstandene Löcher bei den Farbübergängen geschlossen werden.

Kordel (optional)

Mit übrig gebliebenem Studiogarn (hier **B**) eine I-Cord über 5 M mit 5mm Spielnadeln herstellen. Sie sollte ca. 228 cm lang werden. Die Enden zusammennähen.

Square 2

The color sequence for Square 2 is as follows: (4 r **A**, 4 r **B**, 4 r **A**, 4 r **C**) 3 times, 4 r **A**, 4 r **B**, 23 r **A**.
Work as for Square 1 adjusting for the color sequence of Square 2.

Finishing

The border is bound off using 4 mm needles and **D** (a non-felting yarn). This pulls in the work — it will not look very nice, but after felting the piece will be flat and have an even edge (see *before* photo).

Starting with Square 2, bind off 3 sides of the square (240 sts) using a 4 mm needle and **D**. Work 5 rows in St st over the last 80 sts and place on holder.

Bind off 100 sts from Square 1 using a 4 mm needle and **D** and cut yarn. Place next 40 sts on holder. Bind off 100 sts as before with **D**. There should be 80 sts left on the needle.

Place 80 sts from Square 2 onto spare needle. With wrong sides of Square 1 and Square 2 facing, do a 3-needle bind off using **D** and 4 mm needles.

The flap is worked in g st using 5 mm needles and *Studio* yarn. Place 40 sts from holder onto 5 mm needle. Work 24 rows in **A**, 4 rows in **C** and 80 rows in **B**. Bind off in **B**.

Weave in ends closing gaps formed by color changes.

Optional cord With leftover yarn (here color **B**), make an I-cord over 5 stitches and using 5 mm dp needles. Work for about 228 cm (90"). Sew ends together.

Filzen

Das Sitzstück und die Kordel in der Waschmaschine mit einem Handtuch bei 60 °C waschen. Das feuchte Strickstück in Form ziehen und flach trocken. Druckknöpfe entsprechend Grafik annähen.

Felting

Place the finished object (including I-cord) in a washing machine with a towel and wash at 60°C. While still damp, pull into shape and dry flat. Sew snap fasteners as indicated on the diagram.

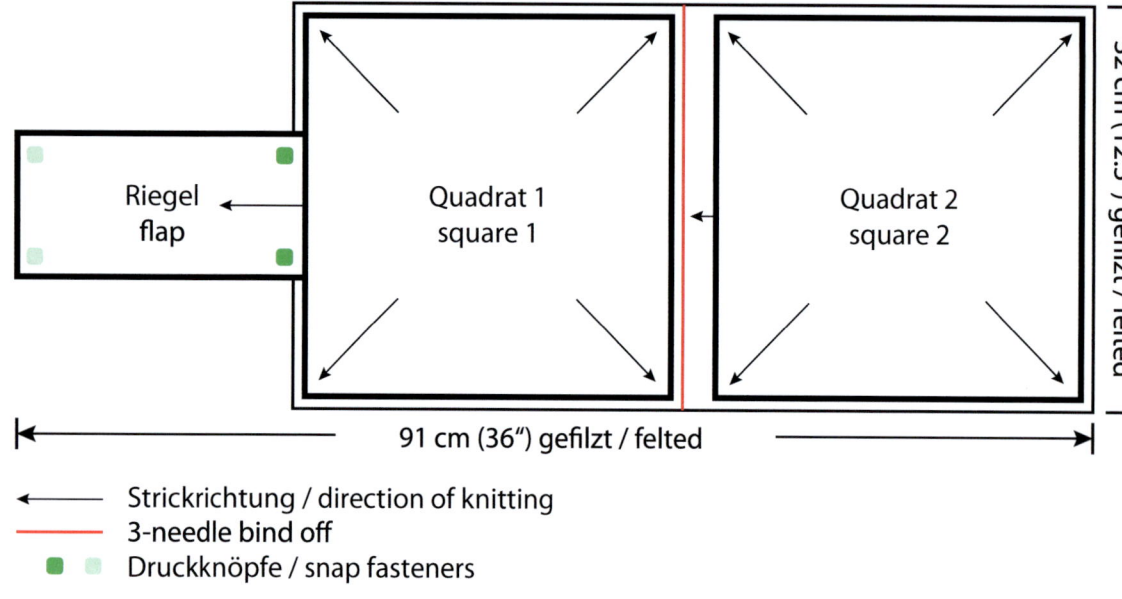

Riegel
flap

Quadrat 1
square 1

Quadrat 2
square 2

32 cm (12.5") gefilzt / felted

91 cm (36") gefilzt / felted

⟵ Strickrichtung / direction of knitting
── 3-needle bind off
● ● Druckknöpfe / snap fasteners

vor dem Fllzen / before felting

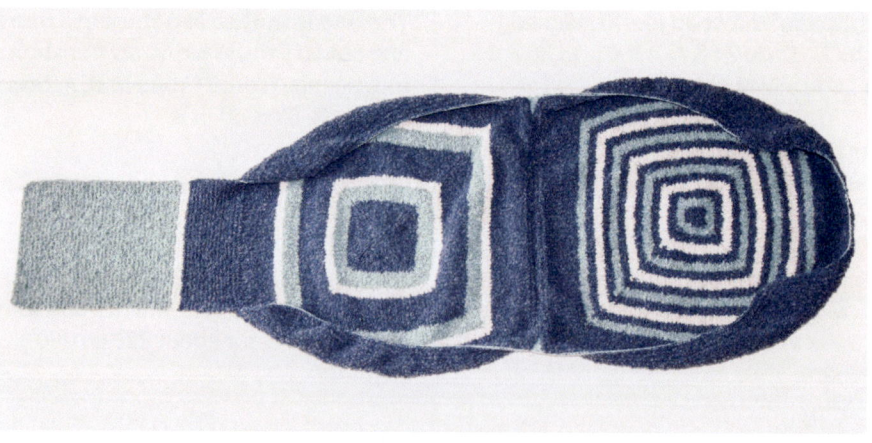

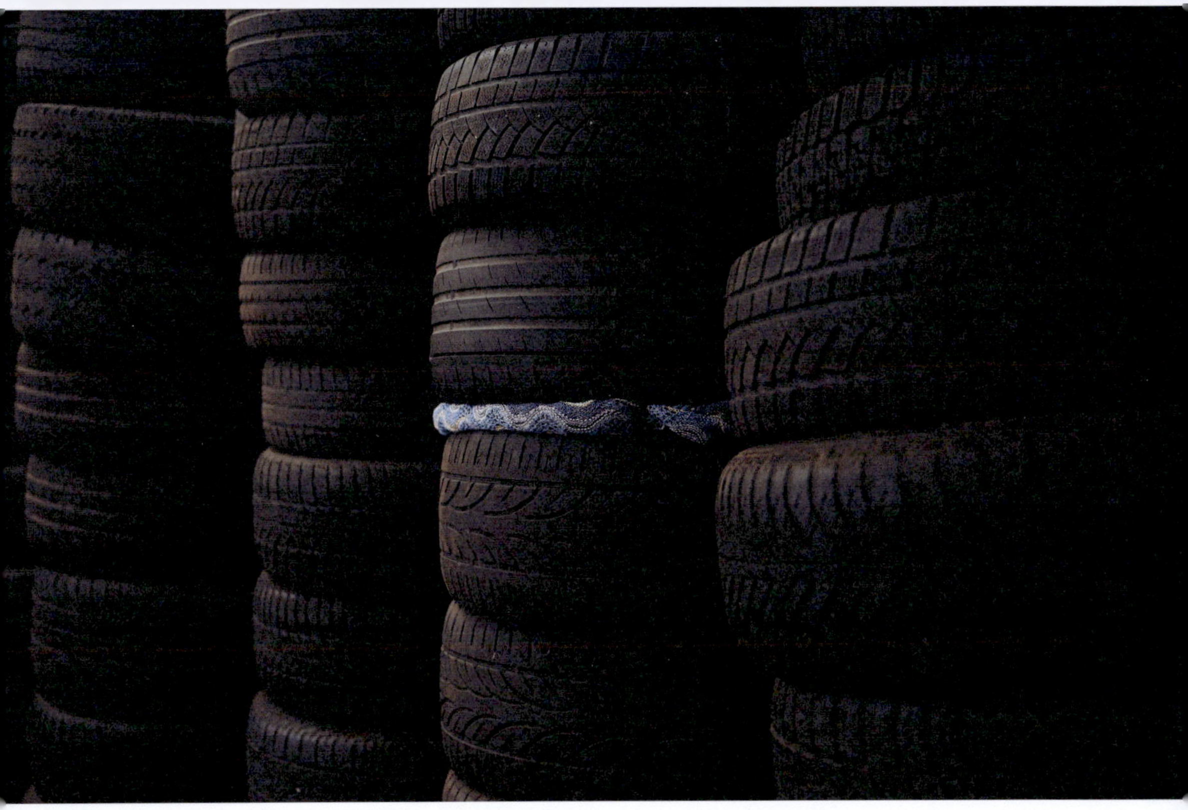

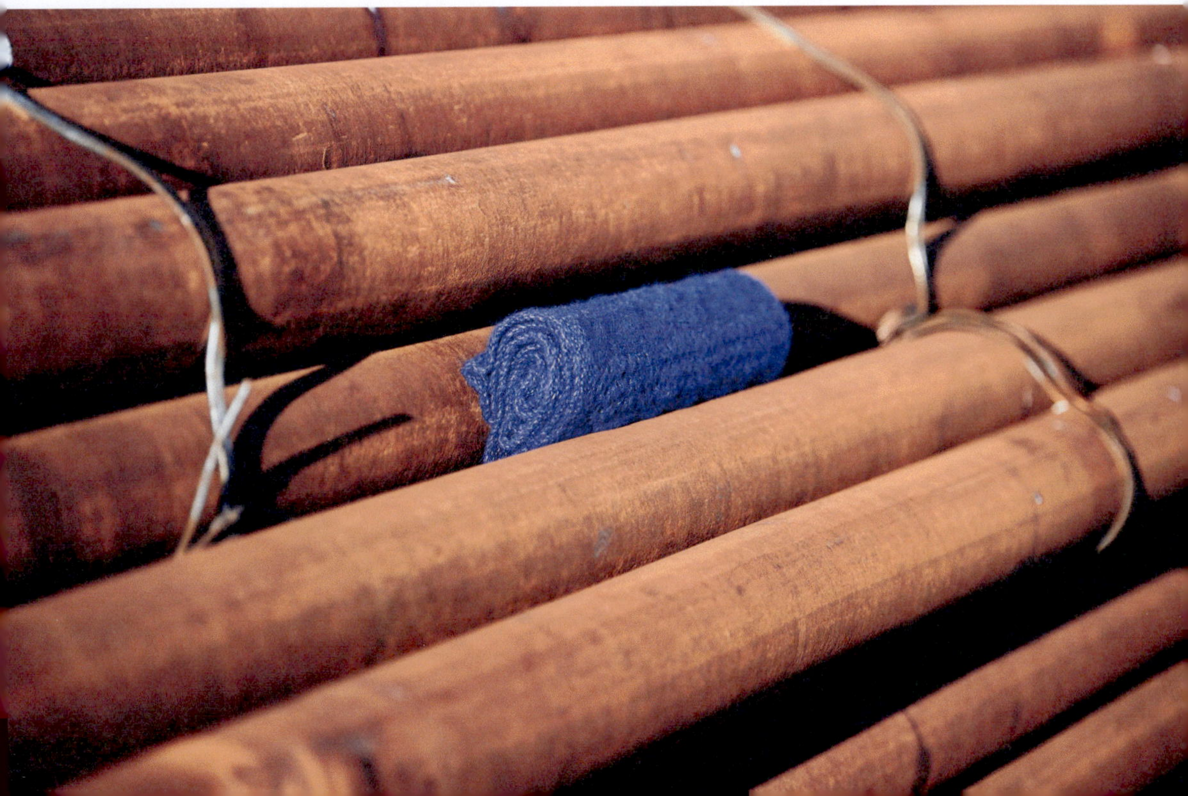

mavi

Schnell und einfach gestrickte Gästehandtü-
cher aus einem Baumwoll/Leinen-Gemisch
verleihen Ihrem Heim das gewisse Etwas.

Quick and easy handmade cotton/linen guest
towels add a special touch to your home.

Lachiwa Mirasol 112m (122yd) / 50g
60% Baumwolle, 40 Leinen
60% cotton, 40% linen

Endgröße 23,5 x 33 cm.

Material Lachiwa, je 1 Strang in Fb.1400 weiß, Fb.1401 hellblau, Fb.1407 pastellblau.

Nadeln Rundstricknadel 2,5 mm, 60 cm lang; Häkelnadel 3 mm.

Maschenprobe 21 M x 38 R = 10 x 10 cm im Perlmuster.

Muster

Perlmuster (ungerade Maschenzahl)
Jede Reihe: RM, *1 M li, 1 M re, von * wdh, 1 M li, RM.

Großes Perlmuster: (ungerade Maschenzahl)
R 1: RM, *1 M li, 1 M re, von * wdh, 1 M li, RM.
R 2: RM, M stricken wie sie erscheinen, RM.
R 3: RM, * 1 M re, 1 M li, von * wdh, 1 M re, RM.
R 4: wie R 2.
Reihen 1 - 4 wdh.

3/3 Schachbrett: (teilbar durch 6 + 2 M)
R 1: RM, *3 M re, 3 M li, von * wdh, RM.
R 2 + 3: RM, M stricken wie sie erscheinen, RM.
R 4: RM, *3 M re, 3 M li, von * wdh, RM.
R 5 + 6: RM, M stricken wie sie erscheinen, RM.
Reihen 1-6 wdh.

Anleitung für weißes Handtuch
49 M anschlagen und so lange im Perlmuster stricken, bis noch ca. 5 m Faden übrig sind. Nun alle M im Muster abketten. Dann den Aufhänger anhäkeln (siehe unten).

Anleitung für hellblaues Handtuch
55 M anschlagen und so lange im großen Perlmuster stricken, bis noch ca. 5 m Faden übrig sind. Nun alle M im Muster abketten. Dann den Aufhänger anhäkeln (siehe unten).

Measurements 23.5 x 33 cm (9.25 x 13").

Yarn *Lachiwa*, 1 skein each in colors #1400 white, #1401 light blue, #1407 pastel blue.

Needles 2.5 mm: circular 60 cm (24"); 3 mm: crochet hook.

Gauge 21 sts and 38 rows = 10 cm (4") in seed stitch.

Stitches

Seed stitch (uneven number of sts)
Every row ES, *p1, k1, rep from*, p1, ES.

Double seed stitch (uneven number of sts)
Row 1 ES, *p1, k1, rep from *, p1, ES.
Row 2 ES, k the k sts and p the p sts, ES.
Row 3 ES, *k1, p1, rep from *, k1, ES.
Row 4 ES, k the k sts and p the p sts, ES.
Repeat rows 1- 4 for pattern.

3x3 squares (multiple of 6 st plus 2)
Row 1 ES, *k3, p3, rep from *, ES.
Rows 2 & 3 ES, k the k sts and p the p sts, ES.
Row 4 ES, *k3, p3, rep from *, ES.
Rows 5 & 6 ES, k the k sts and p the p sts, ES.
Repeat rows 1 - 6 for pattern.

White towel
Cast on 49 sts. Work seed stitch pattern until about 5 m (5.5 yds) of yarn are left. Bind off in pattern. Crochet loop (instructions below).

Light blue towel
Cast on 55 sts and work in double seed stitch pattern until about 5 m (5.5 yds) of yarn are left. Bind off in pattern. Crochet loop (instructions below).

Anleitung für pastellblaues Handtuch

56 M anschlagen und so lange im 3/3 Schach-
brettmuster stricken, bis nach Beenden einer
„Schachbrettreihe" noch mind. 5 m Faden
übrig sind. Nun alle M im Muster abketten und
Aufhänger anhäkeln (siehe unten).

Aufhänger häkeln

Wenn alle M bis auf die letzte abgekettet sind,
diese auf die Häkelnadel nehmen und 10
Luftmaschen (LM) häkeln. Die LM-Kette mit
einer Kettmasche (KM) in die Handtuchecke
zum Kreis schließen und nun 20 feste Maschen in den Kreis häkeln. Mit einer KM in das
Handtuch enden. Faden abschneiden und
vernähen.

Pastel blue towel

Cast on 56 sts and work 3x3 squares pattern
until about 5 m (5.5 yds) of yarn are left and
ending with row 3 or 6. Bind off in pattern.
Crochet loop (instructions below).

Crocheted loop

After binding off, place last stitch on a crochet hook and make 10 chain stitches. Form a
loop and join with a slip stitch. Work 20 single
crochet stitches in the loop. Close with a slip
stitch. Weave in ends.

Abkürzungen / Abbreviations

Deutsch		English	
re	rechte Masche	k	knit
li	linke Masche	p	purl
M	Masche	st	stitch
R	Runde / Reihe	r	row / round
HR	Hinreihe	RS	right side
RR	Rückreihe	WS	wrong side
Fb.	Farbe	#	color
MS	Markierer setzen / verschieben	pm	place marker
gr	glatt rechts HR re, RR li	St st	stockinette stitch k on the RS, p on the WS
gl	glatt links HR li, RR re	rev St st	reverse stockinette stitch p on the RS, k on the WS
kr	kraus rechts alle M re	g st	garter stich k every row
RM	Randmasche: die letzte M mit dem Faden vor der Nadel li abh, die erste M rever stricken	ES	edge stich k first stitch tbl, slip last st purlwise wyif
U	Umschlag	yo	yarn over
1 M Qzu	1 Masche aus Querfaden herausstricken — mit der linken Nadel von vorne nach hinten den Querfaden zwischen den Maschen auf die linke Nadel heben und dann rever abstricken	M1	make one — make a stitch by moving the left needle from front to back under the strand between the last st and the left needle and then knit into the back of the loop.
1 M verd	Masche verdoppeln — 1 M re stricken aber nicht abheben. Die gleiche M nochmals rever stricken und dann erst abheben	kfb	knit into front and back of stitch (1 st increase).
abh	abheben - M von linker auf rechte Nadel heben, Faden dabei hinter der Arbeit	sl st	slip stitch (slip st from left to right needle with yarn in back of work)
reabh	M abh als würde man re stricken		knitwise - sl st as if to knit
liabh	M abh als würde man li stricken		purlwise - sl st as if to purl
2 Mrezus	2 M rechts zusammenstricken	k2tog	knit 2 sts together
ÜZA	Überzugabnahme - 1M reabh , 1 M re, abgehobene M über die gestrickte heben	skp	slip 1 st knitwise, k1, pass slipped stitch over (1 st decrease)
2 Mreverzus	2 Maschen nacheinander re abh, einzeln zurück auf die linke Nadel setzen und dann revers zusammenstricken	ssk	slip 1 st knitwise, slip 1 st knitwise, place tip of left needle through front of these 2 sts from left to right, knit these 2 sts together (left slanted decrease)
	mit Faden vor der Nadel	wyif	with yarn in front
rever	rechts verschränkt stricken	tbl	through the back loop
	zusammen	tog	together
abk	abketten	psso	pass slipped stitch over
wdh	wiederholen	rep	repeat